T0334973

SPORTS ENTREPRENEURSHIP

SPORTS

ENTREPRENEURSHIP

BEYOND THE BIG LEAGUES

CHRISTOPHER MUMFORD

Columbia Business School
Publishing

Columbia University Press
Publishers Since 1893
New York   Chichester, West Sussex
cup.columbia.edu

Copyright © 2023 Columbia University Press
All rights reserved

Library of Congress Cataloging-in-Publication Data
Names: Mumford, Christopher, author.
Title: Sports entrepreneurship : beyond the big leagues / Christopher Mumford.
Description: New York, N.Y. : Columbia University Press, [2023]
Identifiers: LCCN 2023004284 | ISBN 9780231196109 (hardback) |
ISBN 9780231551649 (ebook)
Subjects: LCSH: Sports—Economic aspects. | Sports administration. |
Entrepreneurship.
Classification: LCC GV716 .M86 2023 | DDC 796.06/8—dc23/eng/20230206
LC record available at https://lccn.loc.gov/2023004284

Cover design: Noah Arlow

CONTENTS

ACKNOWLEDGMENTS

All my success is predicated on the enormously hardworking efforts of my parents—Stephen and Judy Mumford—and my always-supportive wife, Joelle. This is especially the case for this book.

I am grateful to Bernard Bell for both offering me a teaching position in sports entrepreneurship years ago and pushing me to reach beyond the known. His warm friendship helped me along the way. I would like to thank Ted Zoller for having faith in me by offering me my first college teaching opportunity. As a result, I had a midlife epiphany that I enjoyed helping change other people's life trajectories as much as changing my own. I so value advice from Don Rose and Jim Kitchen, who have gear that I will never have. Matt Estes remains my greatest mentor and friend in the art and science of startups.

I would like to thank my writing assistants, Joe Taylor and Katie Houston. A special shout-out to Alex Bianchi, who brought so much energy to researching the essential details of the book.

Finally, I so appreciate Myles Thompson, my editor, who turned a lovely dinner conversation into a real book on sports entrepreneurship. I am grateful to Brian Smith for making it real.

PREFACE

My sister and I didn't look like the other kids. I never really felt that I belonged. Sports changed everything for me.

I was that chubby ten-year-old who was always picked last. I enjoyed eating Hostess cupcakes and watching the TV show *Batman* more than running around. My Taiwanese mother thought that sports were a waste of time and a distraction from the all-important studying. My father worked lots of hours. We were poor. During the 1970s, my parents did not draw from parenting templates or books as they did not exist.

My father did think team sports were important. I played T-ball even though I was not very good. My clearest childhood memories include playing catch in our narrow side yard with my father. He threw sidearm because of repeated shoulder injuries from high school football at Manual High School in Louisville, Kentucky. He turned down a football scholarship from the University of Kentucky because of his bum shoulder. Several of his high school teammates later played in the NFL. My dad, sister, and I enjoyed fishing and eating sweets. He did not care for playing board games or any games for that matter.

Because of my weight and lack of interest in running, I became a catcher. My inability to hit the ball well continued from T-ball to baseball.

However, I could catch the ball and had enough of an arm to scare runners from stealing a base. I got all sorts of hitting advice; none of it worked. I practiced at the batting cages. It just confused me more.

During the playoffs, one hitting coach suggested that I shorten my swing and count to two before I swung. Batting eighth, I hit a falling-dove double into shallow right field; a runner scored, to the great surprise of my coach, teammates, and parents. We were down 2–1. In my next at-bat, the pitcher threw a couple of high balls to tease me into swinging. I imagine that he saw my lack of confidence.

The coach and my parents were set for disappointment as it was the bottom of the order. The pitcher's third throw was high but in the strike zone. I counted to two and swung with a short stroke. The ball knifed through the humid south Texas air well past the outfield fence. It was dead silent as no one—especially me—could believe that I had just hit a home run. I was so excited that I almost ran past my own teammate, who was on second base when I hit the ball. While my teammates and coach cheered loudly, the smile on my old man's face in the crowd filled me with happiness.

That is how I fell in love with playing sports.

My baseball career was cut short when we moved to Chapel Hill, North Carolina. The infrastructure was poor compared to the baseball town of Houston. I drifted, trying to find my bearings in basketball country. Still pudgy, I tried out for soccer. The math teacher-turned-coach asked us to separate into two groups: field players and goalkeepers. He yelled at the field players to start running. Given my taste for donuts and dislike for running, I stepped into the goalkeeper line. For the first season, I had only two things going for me: foolish courage and some athleticism. I wasn't afraid to get in the middle of things, largely because that is what catchers do. At the end of the season, I was starting, and we won the conference. I was hooked. I had found my tribe with a unified focus. I had found my place in a new town. I developed a sense of purpose and identity. The game rewarded those who worked hard.

I committed myself to the idea of playing college soccer even though I did not know of anyone who had. Back in those days, if you wanted to learn how to play goalkeeper, you bought a book. A German exchange student, Matthias Karst, sent me a game tape and a fire-engine-red goalkeeper jersey. I watched the saves in that game forty to fifty times while wearing out the elbow pads on the jersey. I trained in my front yard in the August heat. The neighbors thought I was nuts.

Hard work and luck really paid off. My high school team advanced to the state finals so we could get thrashed 5–1. Ouch! I did not like getting five goals scored on me. I doubled down in my training. During my junior year, we won the state championship. As luck would have it, we had nine seniors on the team.

During that season, I was recruited to play on a U30 Olympic Development Team, which was primarily former college stars. Everything was faster and meaner. They took me to the next level. I learned how to anticipate and act faster because I did not have their physical speed. Some teammates were good to me. Some scared me. They were great role models in what not to be: potheads and cocaine users, heavy drinkers, and womanizers. Even at seventeen years old, I quickly saw the downsides to fast living; these players were amazing on the pitch, but some struggled in life. It was a different time. I had to learn how to meet people where they were, not where I wanted them to be. I realized that the story between my ears might not reflect reality.

During that time, I was asked to coach goalkeeping by the insightful, talented Michael Brown. At first, I did it to get paid and earn some recognition. I came to realize that I really enjoyed coaching and teaching. Years later, I realized this experience was the first glimpse of one of my true callings—teaching.

My college experience was chaotic. I didn't know anyone who played college ball. I was clueless. I chose my hometown school.

Carolina men's soccer was not the powerhouse it is today. During my college years, the men's soccer program was in transition. It was a *Lord of the Flies* environment. There were coaching changes and fights between players. Darren Royer, the national team goalkeeper, was one of the players I liked the most. He was also a better goalkeeper than I was. For three years, I tried to outwork him, but, in the end, hard work did not overcome all those years of high-level experience he had. That was a harsh lesson for me. Hard work does not always pay off.

I probably played longer than I should have. I believed in the myth that winners never quit and quitters never win. Said another way, don't change your ways even if things aren't working out. I was gutted. In wanting to get away from it all, I went to Alaska to do commercial fishing during the summer. All those *Most Dangerous Catch* stories are true. If the sea storms didn't kill you, then the bar fights or grizzly bears could get you. I came to realize that I had better improve my grades as real work is damn hard. I also saw former college stars struggle mightily in life after soccer.

I dreaded going back to soccer training. I had maxed out, a realization that every athlete has to make at some point. Finally, I made the decision to move on from the sport and tribe that gave me my sense of self-worth and focus in my formative years. It was my most difficult decision and one that I regretted for many years.

When I got back to campus, I started a race relations group, largely because my university experience was more segregated than my high school experience. I started a philosophy discussion group and political magazine. I worked at a movie theater and coffee shop to pay the bills.

During my senior year, I still had no clue what to do for a job after I finished college. My grades had picked up, and I was doing interesting work on campus, given my newfound freedom. I tagged along with some fraternity brothers to an investment banker recruiting event. I had no idea what investment bankers did. I did not know the difference between net sales and net profits. I had no expectations.

However, to my finance-studying fraternity brothers' surprise, and mine, I got the interviews. I quickly found out that interviewers didn't care so much about what I studied, given that my grades fit into their range. They didn't ask about income statements. They asked what it was like being a soccer player and about my on-campus activities. More importantly, they asked me what it was like being a commercial fisher-man. They wanted the dirt on the danger, drugs, and crazies that I met. I got offers, lots of them. Because of those experiences, I suddenly became the son that my Chinese mother always wanted to have: an investment banker.

It took me many years to unpack how sports impacted my life trajec-tory. During my twenties, I had recurring dreams about going back to Carolina and playing soccer. But the truth is that I had to excel in soccer to develop confidence, grit, anticipation, and management reps. I also had to fail in soccer to drive me to extraordinary experiences, which made me very different from my competition in life. To quote Carolina alum Michael Jordan, "You have to fail in order to succeed." My failure in soccer put me on a completely different life trajectory; now I wake up every morning and work like hell to turn my dreams into reality. I feel so rich to have the freedom to work on the projects for which I have great passion.

Over 98 percent of high school athletes fail to make it to the profes-sional ranks. The 2 percent who do make it to the pros usually last for three to five years. Even the super talented, lucky ones have finished their pro career in a decade. I imagine that, if you are reading this book, then you love your sport. No matter what level you finished playing, you are passionate about teamwork, competition, and effort. You may not be able to follow your original dream, but it can evolve into the dream of creating a sports startup. That is why I wrote this book.

I'm in the game. What is your passion? Do you want to be in the game? If so, then there is one fundamental question that you need to answer.

SPORTS ENTREPRENEURSHIP

Introduction

Now is the greatest time in human history to start a sports business. But it's hard. It's really, really hard. We need to answer the fundamental question of this book: Is the juice worth the squeeze?

Years ago, I was advised to stay away from passion projects if I wanted to make money. As the years passed, I realized that my life was much richer because I did pursue my passion projects. Sports entrepreneurship often starts out as a passion project; it then develops into a hobby. If you work hard and are lucky, it develops into a side hustle. For a very few, a growing, sustainable business develops.

COVID-19 changed everything. The virus forced a hard reset on nearly all sports businesses and remains both the terminator and accelerator of trends. Certain business models will finally fail post COVID-19, while other trends will work extraordinarily well. As the economy recovers, the conditions for starting sports businesses have never been better because of changes in mindsets and the competitive landscape.

Here is why the present is the best time. The cost and barriers of starting a new business are the lowest they have ever been. You can develop and leverage networks inexpensively. The process for starting a new business is much better understood and easy to document. You can test, fail, and repeat quickly and inexpensively without catastrophic outcomes.

Let's put sports into context by looking at traditional subcategories of the industry. According to Richard K. Miller & Associates, U.S. sports annual revenue estimates are greater than $431.5 billion. The largest segments include sports advertising, sporting goods, professional sports, sports travel, and fitness and health clubs (see figure 0.1).

Over 86 percent of Americans consider themselves sports fans, according to the Center for the Digital Future (www.digitalcenter.org) at the University of Southern California Annenberg School for Communication and Journalism. Eighty-eight to eighty-nine percent of sports fans follow more than one sport and more than one team. Over 24 percent of fans self-describe as "intense." The "intense fan" demographic profile is a 35–54-year-old married African American man who has a college degree and an annual salary of $75,000 to $100,000.

See figure 0.2 for the Harris Poll's findings on favorite sports among those eighteen and older.

Scarborough Research (www.scarborough.com) reports that men represent about 66 percent of fans and women about 33 percent in most college and professional sports.

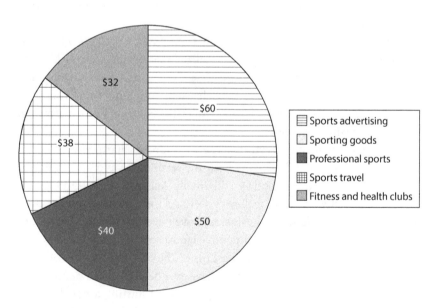

Figure 0.1.
U.S. sporting goods, largest segments ($ in billions).

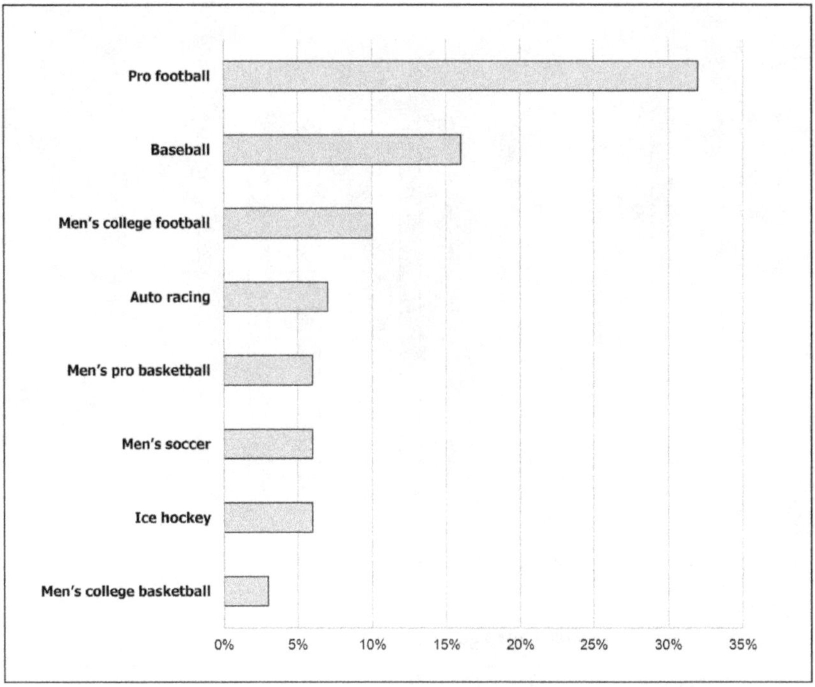

Figure 0.2.
U.S. favorite sports (among people over eighteen years old).

The median household income and average age of people who say they are fans of particular sports, according to Magna Global and *Sports Business Journal*, is shown in figure 0.3.

In this book, we're going to explore areas of high growth. I'm not going to talk about how to become the next owner of an NBA, MLB, or NFL franchise. Unless you have a billion dollars in the bank, those opportunities do not exist. Nor is this book solely for wealthy retired pro athletes, though they could benefit from the book as much as anyone else. We will explore six areas of high growth—analytics, sports betting, eSports, youth sports, fitness and health, and enhanced fan engagement. These areas will dramatically change how sports are played and experienced. The goal of the whole process is to find your signal in the noise of potential opportunities.

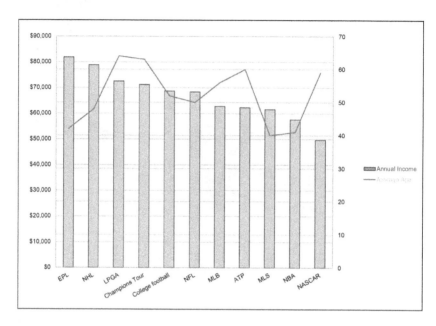

Figure O.3.
U.S. household income versus average age.

Figure O.4.
The sports entrepreneurship ecosystem. Circle size reflects the size of the current market.

Chapters 1 to 6 will develop your subject matter expertise.

Analytics

Depending on the sport, there are great opportunities in data capture, collection, analysis, visualization, and workflow implementation for on-field and in-business operations.

Sports Betting

This segment will grow dramatically as more states legalize mobile betting choices. While the sportsbook-making segment is wrapped up, there are lots of ancillary services to offer.

eSports

The number of video game competitions will increase and advertisers will see a growing number of viewers. Service opportunities are presenting themselves.

Youth Sports

New club opportunities will present themselves as the segment is restructured following the pandemic. Personalized supplemental training will continue to boom.

Fitness and Health

This evergreen segment will reward nimble service providers who can create a specific offering, community, and combined digital and physical presence.

Enhanced Fan Experience

Fan-centric design will drive process improvements in the stadiums, at home, and in mobile app development.

Each chapter is organized into introduction, brief history, key players, constraints, opportunities, personal startup stories, thought leader interviews, and personal startup case studies. The first sections are fairly self-explanatory. The personal startup case studies, presented here with the unvarnished truth, are sports businesses that I started. Some ideas were half-baked. Some are in process. Some failed. Some worked. All were interesting. The thought leader interviews provide insights and real stories on how sports businesses started.

Chapters 7 to 11 describe the process that will help you discover, ideate, validate, and accelerate your dream.

Discover

In the first stage, we evaluate how to align your daily efforts with your main goals. We inventory what you do and what you want to do. In short, we map your reality and sketch out alternative paths to success.

Ideate

We develop a process of creating and crystallizing ideas by developing user profiles and journeys. We map out current best practices and competitors. Most importantly, we get user and stakeholder feedback to understand what's really going on.

Validate

We create and iterate prototypes for users to find a balance between what users are willing to pay and what we can deliver profitably and sustainably.

Accelerate

Once we have a go, we focus on how to grow quickly with promotion and distribution, collateral development, sales management, scaling operations, managing and leading, budgeting, and fundraising.

Personal Startup

It all started with a random question: "What do you want to do next?" I was on the sideline of my son's soccer game with another dad while waves of searing heat emanated from the artificial turf. We were sitting in the shade, away from the yelling parents who dominate youth sports today. I asked the question.

The other soccer dad, Dewan Bader, was a long-time assistant pro coach and even longer time soccer pro. He looked at me and said, "I would like to start a pro soccer team in Wilmington, North Carolina." I did my best not to roll my eyes. The adage is "the only way to make a small fortune in pro soccer teams is to start with a much larger fortune." The only owners I knew lost money and lots of it. But he was serious.

He asked me if I was interested in getting involved. He was the real deal. His parents were both academics; his mom was the first Black woman to earn a PhD at Georgetown. His siblings were all high achievers, yet he chose to join the rough-and-tumble world of pro soccer. His determination shone in his light blue eyes. I liked him a lot, but I said I would pass. As consolation, I invited him to speak at my sports entrepreneurship class about his vision and process.

Several weeks later in class, Dewan spoke about his experiences starting and scaling a youth soccer club before merging with a much larger club. His success was built on player focus, empowering coaches, and being relentless in creating a plucky, competitive club. I asked him to share his vision on creating a pro soccer team. I encouraged the class to take a "Yes and" mindset, like in comedy improv, where you accept your stage partners' suggestions and build on them. We reframed the question to ask what it would take to sustain a pro soccer team in Wilmington. In a rapid-fire Q&A, I saw the first flicker of opportunity despite a business model that did not work, yet. . . .

On the downside, stadium building costs were huge; franchise fees, travel costs, and player and front office payroll were big. With only fifteen home game dates, ticket sales were anemic, sponsorships were a grind, and merchandising meant taking big inventory bets. We built forecast models based on conversations with current teams and the league. Forecast sales were $2 million versus costs of $3.5 million, meaning we had to bridge a $1.5 million gap. Ugh! The numbers did not look good.

Over the next few months, Dewan and I chatted. I wanted to get to know him and see if we were a good fit. In two previous startups, I broke the rule of not trusting my intuition about my partners. Neither one had been a good match, but the opportunities were too appealing. I later came to regret each decision. Choosing your work partner—cofounder—is nearly as important as choosing your life partner. The truth is that you only learn about your potential partners when you run into setbacks. Good times are always easy.

Dewan and I agreed to run through doors until we could not get through. We would pivot as needed. And stop if we could not progress. We reached out to Carson Porter, executive director of the Wilmington Hammerheads Youth Club. As Dewan and Carson had known each other for many years, we had candid conversations about what the youth club wanted from the pro team. A superb player who had coached at all levels, Carson was skeptical as he had experienced the bad side of pro soccer. He had many opportunities to coach elsewhere, but Wilmington was where his heart was. His top priority was developing the community. We dialed in the terms of the relationship. Carson became a champion of the project, introducing us to other local stakeholders—city, potential investors, and former fan groups—so we could understand their needs in the discovery process. The city once had a pro soccer team, Wilmington Hammerheads FC, which played for over twenty years in various pro leagues. Attendance had always been strong, numbering around 2,000 fans per game. The team disbanded in 2017.

We chatted with current pro teams and other sports businesses. The math was pretty simple: grow sales and cut costs. On the revenue side, we took a conservative approach to ticketing and sponsorships. The league averaged 2,200 seats per game; we thought we could do a little better in the first year but not a lot. Sponsorships are hard to win in the beginning if you don't have any actual numbers to support the plan. We did see an opportunity in merchandising if we got our fan engagement and sourcing right.

Based on conversations with league leaders in merchandising, we borrowed best practices and suppliers. After running the numbers again and again, it was obvious that we needed alternative revenue streams. We needed to find sales for more than fifteen home games in a year. We needed a pivot.

We spent a lot of time on other potential products and services. We failed for some time. We narrowed it down to what could we offer on the fifteen game days as well as the other 350 days of the year. I connected the dots when my wife insisted that we stop by a new food hall after our daughter's soccer game. I was blown away by the offering of the six to eight mini restaurants, shared dining area, and full-service bar in an air-conditioned building. The sterile food hall of the 1980s had evolved into something awesome in the 2020s. We started going there after every weekend game. And we were happy to spend lots of money. . . . The value proposition was there. Awesome food and beer in a cool location. Everyone could choose what they wanted to eat.

But here's the catch. Vintage buildings, cooking equipment, and bars cost lots of money to build. The lightbulb went on when I was driving by RTP Boxyard, an outdoor food hall using shipping containers as kitchens. I contacted the shipping container vendor to find out details. Over three months, we were able to price out containers and develop a business model to buy prefabricated kitchens that are 90 percent built out. We would own and operate the bar and coffee shop containers. We would share revenue with food entrepreneurs, who could start with little capital and no long-term leases.

This arrangement aligned with our goals of changing trajectories of people on and off the field. We would provide outdoor screens, covered seating, and a small stage to support local musicians with concerts. We added an outdoor gallery for local artists to showcase and sell their artwork. These elements would broaden our appeal to the public to include sport, entertainment, and arts. And it significantly closed the $1.5 million gap for just pro soccer.

But even that was not enough. We needed another pivot. Getting to cash flow positive in three to four years is acceptable only if there is a pop. Most sports get that pop by selling broadcast rights. We weren't convinced there would be significant sums for another ten years. We canvased again for other revenue streams by seeing what others have done.

We borrowed a play out of the NFL playbook. We looked into developing real estate around the team and stadium. Real estate created that pop in the longer term. Truth is, we did not know much about real estate. But I knew folks who did. In startups, it is mission critical to develop an authentic network of experts. I reached out to my college friend Hector Ingram, who had not lost his English charm after all these years. I pitched the idea to him, and he made some great suggestions. His introductions to real estate developers and owners were the lynchpin of the project. We kept running through doors.

I met with the two largest real estate developers in Wilmington. Both really liked the idea; Raiford Trask responded with greatest enthusiasm. He has an easy drawl and a willingness to try something new. His wife, Eva, won women's soccer NCAA championships at UNC Chapel Hill. We spent seven months preparing for one property his company owned. The 130+ acres were at a great location with a lake. Real estate planning and assessments take much more time than startup time. The main holdup was sufficient road access to the property. I wondered sometimes if we were progressing at all, a pace I find uncomfortable. After all the time invested, we reached a dead end. Raiford and I were crushed. No more pivots here. We could not run through this door.

Before I left town, I called the other developer, Scott Sullivan, who had been kind the first time we talked but seemed less interested. In his modest office, Scott made time for me as I explained the situation and reintroduced the opportunity. With piercing blue eyes and a full head of gray hair, he asked poignant questions in a quiet voice. Our conversation had some uneasy silences on his end, but when I was leaving, he said that one of his properties might be a fit.

A week later, he showed me the 60+ acres his family owned just north of town, not far from the airport. Within a month, a concept map had been created. We could fit an outdoor events space, food hall and beer garden, condos, apartments, and film studios. With the enormous growth of streaming services, there is a shortage of sound stages. Wilmington had already had a film industry for many years with a capable workforce. Neighbors were interested in contributing land if training fields were added. Momentum was gathering.

There were open questions around potential FAA restrictions, road access and flyovers, and power lines. The FAA got back to us quickly, as did the Department of Transportation and power company. No issues with the FAA. The DoT indicated that they had right of way and would likely create an overpass that would bisect the property east to west. In addition, large power lines would bisect the property north to south. Ugh!

Another locked door. It's hard to create a wellness, entertainment, and sport themed property development with power lines and an overpass crisscrossing the property.

Scott called me the next week. He said that he could not find any other viable properties in Wilmington but wondered whether we would consider moving the project twelve minutes west to Leland, a fast-growing area. He said that the property was 1,400 acres, or 2.3 square miles. I looked up the parcel. It was larger than downtown Charlotte!

I asked him what he wanted to do there. Scott answered, "It's simple. I want to build a city." Well, not really a formal city but a very large community with a clear sense of identity, which would be anchored by the outdoor events space with the pro team as the crown jewel. Leland was very supportive. The city could help with building an outdoor events center. Road access was not hard to make but would take some time.

In short, we wanted to create a sustainable community with single family homes, condos, and apartments. The center would be the wellness, entertainment, and sport district. It would include an outdoor events space with a dynamic food hall and beer garden surrounded by retail and health care opportunities. Sports fields, pocket parks, and multiuse trails would create the wellness infrastructure with low-and no-cost programming available to everyone.

Because pro soccer teams on their own are not good businesses, we found other revenue streams—such as a year-round food and beer hall— that could offset expenses. However, community building happens with wellness, entertainment, and sports-themed real estate crowned by a pro soccer team. That combination justifies both town and county support. Stakeholders and potential users found great appeal in the idea of living and working in a place where they could walk to food, sport, and entertainment.

Time will tell as the runway is very long for sports franchises. Setbacks could become dealbreakers. But, for now, we will keep running through doors and pivot as needed.

In retrospect, there are several key takeaways for the Wilmington project ideation: Most passion projects—especially sports-related ones—are hobbies at best. Many people are willing to take low or no rates of return on time and money because they love the concept. That means some unbelievably tough competition where they are willing to play to everyone losing. But you have to have the passion to relentlessly run through doors even when it doesn't seem to make sense. Sometimes the core business does not make sense. You will likely have to change the game or how things are being done. At a minimum, you will have to be 10 percent different. Ask yourself the following questions:

1. **What other value can you create for users to complement the core business?"** Or what are the side revenue streams that can be created? Research what other sports or businesses are doing. Ask potential users what they want. In Wilmington, we are using the NFL real estate model by developing properties around the stadium. We also want to take the game-day fan experience to the next level with food, beverages, and alternative viewing areas.

2. **How can we ratchet down expenses?** Research best practices elsewhere in data collection and process management. Technology can help you cut costs so you can invest more in people. We talked to other soccer teams and minor league baseball teams to learn their approach, process, and tools.

3. **How can we be agile and authentic?** Most founders have at least a fuzzy idea of what they want to do before they start. They should stay crystal clear on their mission but flexible in what the offer or solution is based on facts from users, stakeholders, and best practices. We pivoted several times after getting to know the reality of the situation. Be prepared to pivot to a better idea of the how while staying consistent with the why.

4. **Will I commit to being relentless?** Any business worth doing is damn hard. It will have setbacks. That is normal. There were days when we did not think the project would move forward. We tried to recover faster and harder than the setback pushed us. Bounce back and keep doing the work.

Being relentless is hard. It means putting in the hard work when you are uncomfortable. Throughout the process, regularly check if the juice is worth the squeeze. No doubt the Wilmington project will have twists and turns with unexpected setbacks. It may still fail. But we will continue to run through doors until we cannot.

Let's take a look at the areas that will likely blow up into huge opportunities.

Analytics

Overview

Sports analytics means different things to different people. Some people love the data; most people fear and don't understand them. Sian Beilock, cognitive scientist and president of Dartmouth College, reported in the *Harvard Business Review* that 92 percent of Americans have some math anxiety. Given the general fear of numbers, it's easy to see why most skip over analytics. Winners of games are generally determined by who scores the most points.

But 228 million U.S. drivers rely on analytics in operating their car. How many of them would be willing to have a dashboard with only the number of miles driven; no gas level, engine light, temperature, RPMs, or oil level included. The reality is that most people want information that leads to favorable outcomes like knowing they have enough gas to get home. These "leading indicators" let folks know if they can get from point A to point B.

Sports analytics is no different. Dashboards provide management and coaches with more specific information about what a team needs to do in order to achieve better outcomes. The number of coaches who rely only on the "eye test" and "trusted their gut" is dwindling. It's been a slow decline, but winning matters. Teams who use analytics are winning championships.

Plainly speaking, the general analytics process includes collecting large amounts of information, identifying patterns, and interpreting those patterns to create an impactful subsequent action.

For example, imagine that a coach wants to improve a team's defense against three-pointers. The coach may be able to recall how a particular opposing guard shoots and draw a conclusion.

The sports analytics system may download all the times the opposing guard shot three-pointers and identify that the player shot 10 percent worse when going to the left and another 10 percent worse when forced to dribble more than two times. The coach may instruct his player to overplay his man to force them to dribble to the left. The coach may have been able to draw the same conclusion with the naked eye, but with the use of analytics, these patterns and many more may be identified faster and more effectively.

Analytics is not just limited to the field or court. A business manager may want to identify ways to upsell season ticket holders by using coupons to sell more food and beverages. A fantasy player may want to compare linebacker metrics to select for his fantasy team.

Sports analytics is another tool in the toolbox. Analytics augments the brain rather than replaces it; it is good for describing what reality is—or classifying it—and is possibly helpful in predicting the future. For these reasons, sports analytics has great value in recruiting players, evaluating past performance, and forecasting future performance.

It is unsurprising that the first sport to adopt analytics was baseball. Fans have been tracking box scores—or collecting data—for many years. This DIY data collection was foundational for analytics innovation as the information was publicly available. Other sports have been slower to adopt analytics in part because tracking detailed information was uncommon, while organizational mindsets are slow to change (see figure 1.1). The NBA has followed a course with faster adoption of video technology and relatively fewer players. The NHL has adopted sports analytics along with the NBA for similar reasons. The NFL has been slower to adopt practices as tracking data has been more difficult and the game is more complicated. MLS, and soccer in general, has been the slowest to adopt it due to the lack of data collection, number of players, and continuous nature of the sport.

MAJOR LEAGUE BASEBALL (MLB)

Major League Baseball utilizes a prediction metric called PECOTA, also receiving some criticism due to the volatility of projecting MLB individual performance. With randomness and uncertainty in baseball, predicting a player's season becomes rather complicated, and while PECOTA is the most famous of this group, there is room to grow.

NATIONAL BASKETBALL ASSOCIATION (NBA)

FiveThirtyEight analyst Nate Silver invented the second most famous projection metric called CARMELO in 2015. With CARMELO, the principle is similar to that of VUKOTA where it takes in historical data to identify similar players, and uses their career to forecast a player's future. This metric falls short in failing to account for changes in the style of the game, but it does a good job of encompassing what a projection metric should set out to accomplish.

NATIONAL HOCKEY LEAGUE (NHL)

In the NHL, a website called Hockey Prospectus invented a metric called VUKOTA—a play on MLB's PECOTA—which predicts player performance based on the scoring of historically similar data. This aligns with the purpose of analytics of using historical data to predict the future, though this VUKOTA metric receives significant criticism.

NATIONAL FOOTBALL LEAGUE (NFL)

Football Outsiders created a metric called KUBIAK, which also pays homage to PECOTA in baseball with their projection metric for fantasy football projections. To date, there are not any known publicly available projection metrics.

MAJOR LEAGUE SOCCER (MLS)

With analytics in Major League Soccer being relatively new, there is not yet a fancy modeling system for projecting a player performance across a season. This is likely the most complicated sport to project player performance due to the number of context dependent variables that occur in each play. Further research should be done here.

WHY PROJECTION METRICS IN SPORTS?

There are significant implications of projection metrics in American sports. For starters, it is likely that each organization that relies on analytics implements projection metrics of their own that are proprietary to their respective organization for contract, acquisition, and drafting purposes. In the public space, projection metrics will soon play a role in sports gambling, fantasy sports, and daily fantasy sports.

Figure 1.1.
Projection metrics in major American sports.

Brief History

It is fair to argue that modern sports analytics was grounded in the initial solitary efforts of Bill James in the 1970s. Much of his work is reputed to have been composed during the night shift overseeing the furnaces at the Stokely-Van Camp cannery in Lawrence, Kansas. Given the ample time, he chose to try to answer questions that interested him using data instead of writing about player or coach personalities. During the late 1970s, he sold a few copies of *The Bill James Baseball Abstract*. In hindsight, it seems like it was destined for success. But the truth is acceptance of his work seemed low. He later wrote many annual publications and books. Most went unnoticed for years.

MLB

How could a cannery-working mathematician transform America's game? James's natural curiosity guided him to use data-driven methods to find answers to interesting questions (see figure 1.2). This approach is commonly called sabermetrics, which gets its name from the Society for American Baseball Research (SABR) based in Phoenix, Arizona.

The reality is that pro sports are about winning, which makes and wrecks careers. Brilliantly highlighted by Michael Lewis in his book *Moneyball*, the traditional baseball hierarchy scoffed at new approaches to the sport. As in most innovations, an outsider and a desperate, underperforming enterprise were willing to risk trying something new. The small-market Oakland Athletics—run by the charismatic general manager Billy Beane—embraced sabermetrics to find players who were undervalued by then-traditional baseball metrics. Oakland is now widely credited for consistently making the playoffs despite its comparatively small payroll due to the use of sabermetrics.

The next generation was able to use baseball analytics while adding a large payroll. The result was a World Series winner. Theo Epstein graduated from Yale and had no experience in playing high-level baseball. With no baseball street cred, he started with the Orioles as an intern and followed mentor Larry Lucchino to the San Diego Padres. Epstein

FUNDAMENTALS OF BASEBALL ANALYTICS

An in-depth look into how MLB front offices operate

Coined in 1980 by Bill James, the mathematical and statistical analysis of baseball records became known as "sabermetrics." Sabermetric principles were embraced by Bill Beane during the Moneyball Era, and have subsequently taken the league by storm.

While baseball analytics continues to entail the discovery of undervalued players and competitive advantages, there is a shift toward creating future value. In-game strategy has also seen a shift toward forward-thinking analytical views.

THREE STRUCTURE MODELS

CURRENCY

Runs are the currency of baseball, and players are valued by their contribution to runs as it translates to wins. Metrics include wRC+, wOBA, WAR, and FIP.

CREATION

With increased use of technology to make data analysis possible, MLB front offices are focused on creating optimal development and in game strategies.

PREVENTION

Across all sports, defense entails altering the behavior of the offensive player. In MLB, teams employ shifts to force a hitter to deviate for his strengths, or decrease his likelihood of success when hitting into the shift.

COMPONENTS OF AN MLB FRONT OFFICE

Payroll Rank and R&D Department Size
Plot by @chad_rein | Data: FanGraphs + MLB Media Guides

Focus on the field

Baseball analytics seeks to create unity between the on-field performance and office staff to create more informed decisions.

Balance with tradition

Baseball analytics plans around existing cultural assets, traditional practices, and style.

Appropriate Technology

It emphasizes the employment of building materials systems that are consistent with local contexts such as TrackMan, Edgertronic cameras, and more.

Figure 1.2.
Fundamentals of baseball analytics.

studied law at the University of San Diego to help him with salary contract negotiations. He realized that a law degree was much more credible than analytics at first. At the age of twenty-eight, he was recruited by the Boston Red Sox as general manager in 2002. The Red Sox embraced data-decision recruiting with several key signings and won the World Series in 2004, eighty-six years after their first World Series win. For good measure, the team won again in 2007. Epstein left the Red Sox in 2011 for the Chicago Cubs. In 2016, the Cubs won their first World Series in 108 years.

The adoption of baseball analytics was slow in the early years since the sport was very traditional. However, nearly all teams now use analytics as an important instrument in their toolkit. The Houston Astros were widely credited with using analytics not only for player identification but also for playing tactics by using defensive shifts or positioning. The Astros won their first World Series in 2017. After multiple validations of analytics from various teams, general managers of other sports started to pay attention.

It's fair to say that while analytics is a commonly used tool in major league baseball and major college baseball programs, independent teams often don't have the budget to support an analytics staff.

NBA

Basketball had a slow start to analytics. Coach Frank McGuire of the University of North Carolina used basic possession statistics. In the 1990s, Dean Oliver advanced the concept of possession statistics in basketball. He was eventually hired by the Seattle Supersonics (now Oklahoma Thunder) in 2004. While others contributed to the movement, adoption was slow (figure 1.3). The sport of basketball enjoyed a significant jump in analytics use after the 2013–2014 season. The league installed a video tracking system in each of the arenas to share data with the team. The reality is that faster-moving games—unlike baseball—make it harder to translate individual plays into statistics. Video can be rewound to help analysts "code"—or record—events into data.

Founded in 2013, Second Spectrum helps clients to automatically organize and index plays on the basketball court within seconds. Using the NBA video tracking system, the company created the most advanced

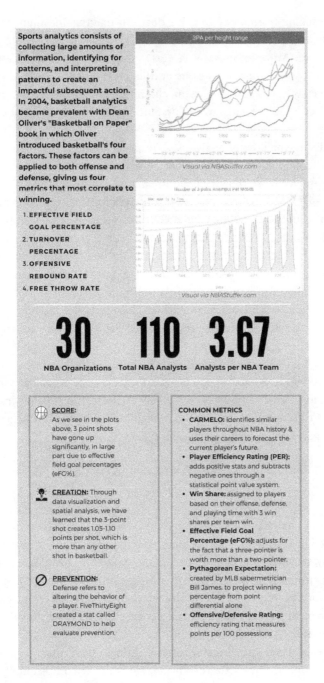

Sports analytics consists of collecting large amounts of information, identifying for patterns, and interpreting patterns to create an impactful subsequent action. In 2004, basketball analytics became prevalent with Dean Oliver's "Basketball on Paper" book in which Oliver introduced basketball's four factors. These factors can be applied to both offense and defense, giving us four metrics that most correlate to winning.

1. EFFECTIVE FIELD
   GOAL PERCENTAGE
2. TURNOVER
   PERCENTAGE
3. OFFENSIVE
   REBOUND RATE
4. FREE THROW RATE

Visual via NBAStuffer.com

Visual via NBAStuffer.com

30
NBA Organizations

110
Total NBA Analysts

3.67
Analysts per NBA Team

SCORE:
As we see in the plots above, 3 point shots have gone up significantly, in large part due to effective field goal percentages (eFG%).

CREATION: Through data visualization and spatial analysis, we have learned that the 3-point shot creates 1.05-1.10 points per shot, which is more than any other shot in basketball.

PREVENTION: Defense refers to altering the behavior of a player. FiveThirtyEight created a stat called DRAYMOND to help evaluate prevention.

COMMON METRICS
- **CARMELO:** identifies similar players throughout NBA history & uses their careers to forecast the current player's future.
- **Player Efficiency Rating (PER):** adds positive stats and subtracts negative ones through a statistical point value system.
- **Win Share:** assigned to players based on their offense, defense, and playing time with 3 win shares per team win.
- **Effective Field Goal Percentage (eFG%):** adjusts for the fact that a three-pointer is worth more than a two-pointer.
- **Pythagorean Expectation:** created by MLB sabermetrician Bill James, to project winning percentage from point differential alone
- **Offensive/Defensive Rating:** efficiency rating that measures points per 100 possessions

Figure 1.3.
Principles of basketball analytics.

player-tracking technology to drive decision-making and higher levels of fan engagement.

The San Antonio Spurs were early adopters of basketball analytics, followed by the Houston Rockets and, later, the Golden State Warriors. Unsurprisingly, these teams won championships largely because they had an extra tool, or lens, to understand reality without all the emotion and bias.

As in baseball, early analytics were used in recruiting players. Daryl Morey, a computer science major at Northwestern who later received an MBA from MIT, is known as a thought leader in basketball analytics. Cochair of the MIT Sports Analytics Conference, Morey is also an avid supporter of eSports and owns Clutch Gaming, a League of Legends eSports team based in Houston.

Basketball analytics has evolved from player recruitment to many other areas, including positional play, scoring opportunities, and optimal matchups, as well as rest and recovery optimization. In 2015, Nate Silver at fivethirtyeight.com introduced CARMELO, a predictive method of valuing players based on previous players' careers. These metrics were applied to create overall team predictions.

Basketball analytics is fairly advanced in the NBA with uneven applications in college basketball and G League. Older coaches, management skepticism, and insufficient budgets will likely be overcome as younger coaches come into the leagues and artificial intelligence drives down the cost of collecting, cleaning, and organizing the data.

NHL

The hockey analytics evolution timeline is similar to the NBA's adoption. In 2015, the NHL announced a partnership with SAP, an enterprise software company, to collect and analyze data. As in basketball, positional and event data is commonly used to evaluate player, tactic, and team classification and prediction (see figure 1.4). However, puck-and-player tracking was slower to be implemented, as contrasted with the NBA's positional tracking implementation in 2013.

Michael Peterson, director of the Tampa Lightning, was another unlikely pioneer of the data revolution. He is the Theo Epstein of hockey analytics. In early 2009, the Lightning general manager charged his staff with finding the "smartest mathematician who was a rock star in his field."

SINCE ITS LAUNCH,

32 TEAMS

All 32 NHL teams have grown analytics departments to keep up with the landscape of the game. Analytics have become commonplace in hockey.

CURRENCY GOALS

Advanced metrics attempt to discover how many goals a player adds. Goals Above Replacement (GAR) measures this specifically, and xG is the expected goals independent of goalie talent or shooting ability.

SCORING CREATION

Corsi: sum of shots on goal, missed shots, and blocked shots. The purpose is to measure the workload of the goalkeeper during a game.
Fenwick: unblocked shot attempts which has a strong correlation to scoring chances.

PREVENTION DEFENSE

Passing data helps determine the defensive ability of an NHL team. If a team is able to determine the pre-puck movement, they can isolate individual performance, team performance, etc. on the defensive side.

APPLICATION: ZONE STARTS

The ratio of how many face-offs a player is on the offensive zone relative to the defensive zone. Players with high zone starts see positive correlation with Corsi, so coaches give players with more zone starts more playing time to create goal scoring opportunities.

Figure 1.4.
Hockey analytics.

At first glance, Peterson did not fit the profile (for example, he had never played hockey in his home state of Texas), but deeper interviews proved different. His earlier work was with the Cleveland Indians and Tampa Bay Rays on how promotions affected payroll. Peterson's work with the Lightning paid off with back-to-back Stanley Cups during the 2020 and 2021 seasons. Latecomers Colorado Avalanche restructured with a much heavier emphasis on analytics during 2017 with a payoff of the Stanley Cup in 2022.

Use of analytics in the NHL will accelerate now that the Stanley Cup has been won by "quant" teams for the last three years.

NFL

Football analytics had its beginning in the early 1970s when Virgil Carter, a Brigham Young star quarterback and later an NFL journeyman with a QB rating of 69.9, wrote the paper "Operations Research in Football" with Robert Machol, a systems engineer. He went to high school in Folsom, California, about four miles from Folsom State Prison, where country singer Johnny Cash spent time and later wrote a song about. In 1998, Carter wrote a book called *The Hidden Game of Football*, which was not even considered by most of the traditional football hierarchy.

Starting in the early 2000s, Warren Sharp began publishing an annual football season preview and maintaining a subscription-service website for fans and sports bettors. He is best described as the Bill James of pro football. ESPN has jumped into the sports analytics revolution by hiring a former Navy F-18 fighter pilot Brian Burke to proselytize and popularize football analytics over recent years. ESPN is a sports storyteller; analytics is another tool to help tell fresh stories daily.

The NFL started tracking player positioning across the league using a system called Next Gen Stats in 2018. Teams are faced with a deluge of information (see figure 1.5). They have staffed analytics departments and work with outside consultants to find the signal in the noise. In due time, this positional tracking system will change football in the same way that the NBA changed.

According to an ESPN survey of NFL analysts, the Cleveland Browns and Baltimore Ravens appear to be investing the most in analytics though the work has yet to show in their recent field performance. The survey

MARKET ANALYSIS

Related to Moneyball in Major League Baseball, teams across all sports are using advanced analytics and metrics to determine the true market value of certain players. Analytics provides front offices with the tools to make informed decisions regarding trading, signing, and drafting players.

COMPETITIVE ADVANTAGE

In baseball, MLB analytics staffs had to convince the coaches to not bunt and give up outs. Similarly, NFL teams are realizing the competitive advantage that arises from holding onto the ball, and thus, not punting. Of six teams with 4th down conversion rates above 70%, five were playoff teams.

SCOUTING ADVANTAGES

Tracking technology is improving decision making with respect to acquiring players. Game speed is different than a 40-yard dash, and closing speed is a new metric to evaluate linebackers. Teams that are able to back up the "eye test" with data have an advantage.

IMPROVED PLAY CALLING

The days of running the ball seem to be behind us. Teams are being more aggressive as it relates to passing the ball, going for it on 4th down, and more. The expected yards per play of a pass is significantly higher than a run, which provides some scientific reasoning here.

TRUE VALUE OF PLAYERS

We are seeing a shift in the value of certain players. For example, we are now seeing more dual-threat quarterbacks than the typical pocket passer. With teams passing more, it makes sense to have that running option to keep the defense off-balanced. They are also working on a Wins Above Replacement metric.

Figure 1.5.
Objectives of football analytics.

indicated that the analytics work has been done in all areas including coaching, pro personnel, draft, game management, and sport science.

In the same survey, the analysts estimated that NFL analytics are at least ten years behind that of the MLB. Some teams, such as the Tennessee Titans, still celebrate being anti-analytics. Time will tell; analytics is still an open question on how big the difference is between what teams say they are doing versus what is actually being done. In the NFL's case, it's not a money thing—it's more a culture and about really understanding the metrics and actions, which are difference makers. Colleges, on the other hand, are more prone to a less adaptable coaching culture since recruitment with traditional schools drives so much of their success.

MLS

Soccer's adoption of analytics has been off to a slow start. Collecting discrete data points is more challenging because the game is continuous in nature. In baseball, you have a pitch, hit, or outfield play. In football, there are about 160 plays per game. In addition, European soccer is very traditional.

There has been meaningful progress in key metrics, such as expected goals and expected assists, but much is still to be desired in terms of precise data capture as well as defining clearly the indicators of goal buildup or prevention (see figure 1.6). Analytics were partially attributable to Leicester City Football Club's amazing Cinderella-story win in the Premier League in 2015–2016.

Liverpool Football Club—recent winners of the Champions League and Premier League—has fully integrated analytics into its soccer operations. It is no surprise that Liverpool FC is owned by Fenway Sports Group, which also owns the Boston Red Sox. Other top-tier clubs have adopted analytics in their player recruitment to differing degrees. The MLS has developed an international reputation for adopting analytics into its operations. College soccer analytics adoption is still in its infancy, relying squarely on eye tests and video analysis.

Soccer analytics adoption—outside of the Big Five European Leagues and MLS—will be hampered by inadequate budgets and the complexity of the game.

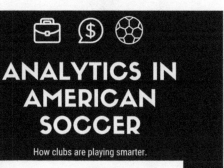

ANALYTICS IN AMERICAN SOCCER

How clubs are playing smarter.

PURPOSE

Strengthen and secure ideas.

Major League Soccer (MLS) is the only major sport league in the United States with an in-depth breakdown of analytics usage in the sport. They have changed the game leading to closer shots, shorter goal kicks, quick throw ins, and more.

INVESTMENT AND INNOVATION

Displaying their vision to be the leader.

Just days before the start of the 2020 season, MLS partnered with second spectrum to improve tracking technology. MLS is making it clear that they are willing to take large strides to become the leader of analytics in American sports.

TRENDS AND OPPORTUNITIES

The soccer world is smaller than ever.

With the growth of data and analytics, MLS clubs are able to make evaluations on players from all parts of the world. Analytics is not replacing scouting, but making it easier backing up eye-tests with data. Another growing part of analytics in soccer is video analyses to go along with advance metrics.

MYTHS

Common myths about soccer analytics.

One of the biggest myths is that soccer analytics is just like Moneyball. While Moneyball was the inspiration for analytics in sports, soccer is very context-depending, and a player has an infinite number of options with or without the ball. This means soccer cannot be 100% quant-minded.

Figure 1.6.
Analytics in American soccer.

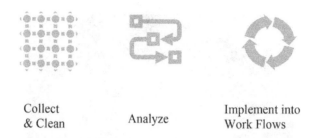

| Collect & Clean | Analyze | Implement into Work Flows |

Figure 1.7.
Data analytics process.

The Data Analytics Process

There are three main steps to sports data analytics, which are illustrated in figure 1.7.

1. Collecting and organizing the data
2. Analyzing it
3. Implementing and applying it successfully

Data Collection

Large amounts of information must be collected and organized in order to identify meaningful patterns. This step has been greatly simplified with the declining cost of computing, video, and sensors and the adoption of databases and spreadsheets. The falling cost of both hardware and software has fueled the revolution during the last decade. In sports, analysts input data points while watching game footage. An analyst records certain data points for every play in every game of the season. The analytics revolution has happened largely because of the video revolution. The data feeds are often available for a monthly fee. The data needs to be transferred from the provider in a CSV file (Excel), XML, or JSON (JavaScript). The latter two are languages by which databases can be transferred efficiently. In other instances, sensors on the athlete relay data via Bluetooth to a database.

Once imported, the data needs to be "cleaned" so that errors or an extra space or comma will not interfere with the next step of analytics.

During the last decade, there has been a great deal of entrepreneurship in sports data collection, including Sportradar, STATS Perform, and MySportsFeed. These companies' relationships with the professional leagues have been turbulent. In some cases, the leagues have sued these companies for intellectual property infringement. Recently, the leagues have entered into agreements with respective companies to be their exclusive sports feed providers. In addition, the leagues have acquired player-worn sensor technologies to track individual player performance in terms of heart rate, positioning, speed, etc. The leagues have strongly favored an "integrity tax" on data feeds. The money would be used to monitor potential game fixing. The reasoning is that sports bettors will be the greatest consumers of the sports data feeds. The leagues want more money to protect the integrity of the game.

The next generation of sports data will be proprietary feeds that capture information that is not currently being used. For example, the NFL has promoted the use of body motion sensors embedded in shoulder pads to create the Next Gen stats database. Currently, much of the data is event data, which are details of a series of events that happen in a game. Positional data will grow more commonplace. A hybrid approach will likely prevail as companies identify unique ways to capture metrics or measures.

Analysis

After the data are imported and cleaned, the information is moved into an analytics model. In sports analytics, the most common uses are for recruiting and prediction. In the case of recruiting, descriptive models are used. For example, an NFL team may want to recruit a safety who is highly effective at preventing deep passes, especially during the second and third downs. They can rank all college senior safeties by these particular metrics.

In the case of prediction, predictive models are used. For example, an NFL team may want to evaluate the effectiveness of passing on the first or second down against a particular opponent. The model will evaluate all outcomes when teams run passing plays in those situations. Moreover, a model could run multiple simulations to determine the success probabilities. In addition, a pro hockey team ticket manager may want to forecast the effectiveness of a ticket bundle to encourage attendance against low-ranked opponents.

Fundamentally, analytics is the science of understanding how one variable relates to other variables. The field of data science, which uses both traditional regression and more novel machine learning, is growing tremendously in all areas. Most coaching and analytics staff are guarded about sharing their analytical techniques for competitive reasons. Therefore, it's hard to know where they stand in implementing analytical models. Meanwhile, the front office, or business side, of most professional organizations share best practices as they serve their own markets. These practices are often in line with the best practices of other business organizations in terms of customer relationship management, marketing, and operations analytics.

Daily fantasy sports (DFS) players will use websites like Next Gen Stats or the subscription model Pro Football Focus to access data that uses either unique data feeds or algorithms. There is a growing DIY data analytics movement where people buy their own data, run their own algorithms, and apply predictions to DFS or sports betting.

Implementation

Once the models are run, the results must be interpreted to understand how to apply the information to the users. Several questions need to be answered:

1. **How do the results compare to current thinking?** It is critical for the analyst to discuss results with coaches to determine if the insights can be used in real conditions, in part because not all of the needed inputs were captured in the data feed. It is important to consider the eye test or traditional wisdom perspective.

2. **Are the results easy to understand?** Non-data analysts tend to freeze up if shown a full page of numbers. The data must be

presented in a visually appealing way in order to get traction. Story-telling with data and graphical representations is a fast-growing area with best practices crystallizing now.

3. **How do reporting results fit into traditional workflows?** The key is to incorporate with ease the analytics into the regular schedule and processes of the users (coaches and office staff). Coaches in particular will not likely include results if doing so creates much more work for them.

4. **Does the organization have the right resources to implement the insights and give feedback?** The organization must have the right people and infrastructure to use the insights. This fit is essential for success. In addition, a process must be in place to capture feedback once the insights are implemented. Successful analytics deployment depends on improvement based on multiple iterations.

5. **Does analytics have support from top to bottom of the organization?** Successful analytics implementation depends on buy-in from the owner, who dictates to the general manager and coach the importance of analytics in the toolkit. An organization will not be successful without the proper mindset at all levels.

6. **Does the analytics support the organization's philosophy?** The goal is not necessarily to find the best players or tactics but to find the players or tactics that best fit the team philosophy. Analytics should help the organization be different, as most teams will chase the best players or tactics.

Key Players

Leagues

The professional leagues have wised up to the fact that game data is important and can be sold. Each league has websites that present basic stats. While there were some legal conflicts in the past, leagues have entered into multiyear deals with sports data feed companies, primarily Sportradar. The leagues have different tiers of data. While much data is available to the paying public, an advanced tier of data is only shared with the teams. These lines are constantly changing, given the improvements in data capture and team ownership acceptance.

Broadcasters

Leagues make big money selling broadcast rights—namely televising games and selling advertising. Traditional TV companies—CBS, NBC, ABC, and Fox—dominated sports entertainment for years. Cable companies crept in next, but the large streaming services (Amazon, Apple, and Disney) have flooded the market and driven up pricing. Direct-to-fans internet companies such as Fubo are the next wave, likely for smaller leagues. Leagues have begun selling data rights separately, but the biggest check-writing broadcasters want to continue to bundle broadcast and data so they can provide data-intensive offerings online.

Data Providers

These companies collect and analyze data and resell it to teams, media, sportsbooks, and bettors. The largest players are Sportradar and STATS Perform. Created in 1981, STATS was the first mover in sports data collection. In the 1990s, the company was the official data provider for the NFL, NBA, and NHL. In addition to data, they provided articles to the Associated Press and Yahoo Sports.

Though they have lost official data provider status with most U.S. professional leagues, STATS collects its own data and provides value-added services of analytics and content. Founded in 2003 in Switzerland, Sportradar is one of the biggest sports data companies, and it is backed by investors Michael Jordan, Mark Cuban, and the NFL. They were the official data provider for the NFL, NHL, NBA, MLB, and NASCAR. Sportradar has launched ad:s, a sports betting marketing firm. Having made its name in basketball, Second Spectrum greatly expanded the depth of plays and indexing using AI. For example, they have identified over sixty different types of pick and roll. Their strength is in having AI capture motion. They have expanded into player movements using stick figures based on textiles that have motion tags to better understand positioning. The company has since expanded into MLS and EPL. Publicly traded Genius Sports acquired Second Spectrum for $200 million in mid-2021.

These companies are moving toward providing broader solutions for their clients. A large number of smaller sports data companies serve DIY sports analysts, sports bettors, and smaller-scale media. One novel approach is MySportsFeed, which offers crowd-sourced stats to the DIY sports analytics community.

Technology Companies

Companies such as IBM, SAP, and SAS got involved initially as hardware suppliers, transitioned to software providers, and currently are data collection and analysis cloud platforms. These companies will continue to get more involved as position data will require more robust analytics collection using traditional AI and machine learning.

Teams

In terms of recruiting, identifying opponent weaknesses, and making predictions, the most obvious users of analytics are general managers, coaches, scouts, and analysts. Depending on the sport, the adoption rate varies from complete acceptance to simply paying lip service. Often bringing in outside consultants, teams are very secretive about their actions. On the business side, sales and marketing staff have warmly embraced customer relationship management (CRM) data collection for fan recruitment and retention. Different teams' marketing departments will share best practices as they operate in different geographic areas.

Media

Websites, TV, and print media will buy data as well as accompanying analysis and content so they can use it in their programs and publications. In addition to traditional sports media such as ESPN and CBS Sports, sports analytical media like Pro Football Focus will create paid subscriber-only products for teams, agents, DFS, and super fans. Expect the media to purchase analytics companies or their staff.

DFS

Fantasy players are a rapidly growing segment that consumes data and media. Based on the data and their analysis, they form their own teams for varying time periods.

Sports Betting

Sportsbooks—both domestic and offshore—are large consumers of data and content, which allows them to establish betting lines and create more content to take bets. Handicappers follow the sportsbooks and consume data and content. Sports bettors consume data and content in an effort to find that edge. This segment will likely grow dramatically.

Constraints

ACCESS TO INTELLECTUAL PROPERTY Data collected from traditional video analysis is commonly available to any data provider willing to invest the time to track the plays. However, only the official data provider has access to multicamera angles or body-worn sensors. Teams want to have some control over key data. It is very challenging for newcomers to get access to these proprietary data streams. Analytics improvements usually develop more rapidly when data is available to the public since teams are reluctant to share their findings for competitive reasons.

CAPITAL Doing business with the pro leagues requires scale. The leagues want multiyear, multimillion-dollar contracts. Leagues—that have much to lose in a misstep—are conservative with the company they keep.

DATA ANALYTICS EXPERTISE This is obvious. The industry standards change very quickly as the space moves from traditional rules-based AI to machine learning.

DETERMINING A SIGNAL FROM THE NOISE The amount of data is overwhelming, especially with the dramatically falling prices of sensors. It's challenging to structure the data and get actionable conclusions.

NUMBERS VERSUS PEOPLE MINDSET There is still a prevailing mindset that analytics will replace human judgment. The reality is that data analytics is a tool to augment human decision-making by providing a different take on what reality is. This mindset has largely changed in baseball and basketball. Much more education is needed for hockey, football, and soccer. There is also a steep learning curve for fans though fantasy sports have done a great deal to educate the public.

Opportunities

You will face an uphill battle if you join the sports analytics segment.

Analytics in sports is like getting your car serviced or going for your annual medical screening. Everyone knows you should do it, but no one likes to do it or pay for it. However, we get upset when our car breaks down on a long trip even though we don't regularly get it serviced. Sports managers and coaches tend to be very traditional and find it hard to adopt new ideas.

Sports decision-makers have the same bias as everyone else—they think information and statistics should be free. The internet model of paid advertising for "free information" is what leads to that bias. Information is thought of as a commodity. However, the added value comes from knowing what the relevant information is and how to use it. I have met with large sports organizations with revenues in excess of $100 million. They are collecting enormous amounts of data in several databases. However, the databases are integrated, and the staff doesn't know how to access information from several of the databases. There are no dashboards or systematic key performance indicators. This scenario is reminiscent of where midsize businesses were in the 1990s or where investment banks were in the 1980s. Today, it would be inconceivable for financial traders not to have robust trading analytics platforms. As professional sports organizations commit half a billion dollars for ten-year player contracts, well-thought-out analytics will be the necessity, not the exception.

The growth of the sports analytics field is stunted by the fact that teams or their consultants don't share their methods or research. This is understandable as teams need to win by using every competitive advantage. Oftentimes, innovation comes from newcomers in the field willing to share their methodologies on blogs and Twitter. When recognized, they are often hired by teams or consultancies where they are not allowed to publish their findings. It is the opposite of science in terms of publishing and sharing information so others can build more quickly on preexisting research. For those that want to get into sports analytics, publish work on blogs and Twitter to develop a reputation for your work. You will be found.

Sports analytics will be more highly valued by organizations when the sports fan becomes more knowledgeable about analytics. Baseball is an example where fans are more knowledgeable in analytics than are fans of most other sports. DFS and sports betting are educating the next generation of fans through their platforms. This growing level of sophistication will compel sports organizations to become more aggressive in analytics, according to Garth Lagerway, GM of the Seattle Sounders MLS team.

Organizations currently have a low-value perception of sports analysts. The new analysts are often paid very little, and the departments are the first to get fired in a slowdown. There is often a clash of mindsets—the statheads versus the "real" sports guys. However, change is happening. Billy Beane estimates that of the thirty baseball teams, only two general managers come from a traditional baseball background like himself. He joked that he would not be able to get a GM job today. Goldman Sachs and McKinsey are his competitors to hire analytics talent.

In truth, the trend is your friend. Outcomes matter in sports. Consider the following fairly recent winners of different sports: Boston Red Sox, Chicago Cubs, Houston Astros, New England Patriots, Golden State Warriors, Chicago Blackhawks, Tampa Lightning, Colorado Avalanche, Seattle Sounders, Atlanta FC, Leicester City FC, and Liverpool FC. The common denominator is that analytics were implemented in each team's decision-making toolkit. It is not the sole tool but an important way of seeing reality for what it is. Results matter.

Here are where the opportunities lie . . .

PROPRIETARY DATA Depending on the sport, these feeds will include data not used by competing organizations. There are possibilities for startups to develop these specialized data sources to resell. Additional metrics could be athlete mental makeup, family history, and team chemistry measures. Let's look at other industries. In finance, the proprietary data revolution already happened. These alternative data streams serve as different lenses of what reality is. For now, game video is viewed and analyzed by a team of analysts in a room. Going forward, AI is going to take over the lion's share of that grunt work while analysts focus more on consistency and better understand exceptions. There is room for this blending of human and machine capture and analysis.

ANALYSIS There are opportunities to build better algorithms, particularly as we move into the machine learning revolution. The applications are for both uses by teams and consumers, particularly DFS and sports betting. More importantly, there is likely a greater opportunity to successfully apply existing algorithms in existing or new data feeds. This pattern has already emerged in financial trading and business analytics.

CONTENT PROVIDERS There is a considerable opportunity to make sports analytics easier to understand and consume. Enterprises will prosper if they can educate users and provide easy-to-understand visualizations and easy-to-follow recommendations. Winners will include those that make it easier for the impending huge growth of new sports bettors and DFS players. However, sports analytics providers have learned that narrative-plus-analytics is needed to drive usage, especially for consumer subscription models. In the end, consumers want to hear more stories supported by stats and tactics. Time will tell if traditional content providers pivot to using data-informed storytelling or whether new entrants will flourish. There is a narrow space between data providers and the ruthlessly competitive traditional content providers.

CONSULTING Most professional teams have in-house analytics staff or exclusive consulting support. Implementation at colleges and high schools was tried early on but has been a mixed bag at best. Even the top-tier NCAA university usage is spotty. Soccer academies are employing in-game analytics tracking, but the only consulting widely available is that from data analytics companies like InStat and Wyscout. Over time, the traditional consulting companies will get into this space since it requires a similar framework that they currently use with midsize companies. However, professional and particularly college organizations are not willing to pay consulting company rates. There is a window for more flexible, lower-cost entrants to win business and establish credibility.

Personal Startup

I'm not a numbers guy even though I was an investment banker and CFO. Deep down, I am a philosopher looking for meaning. My brain is built for processing stories—like most every human—but I realize that I have to use data to believe the right narrative, which I call real reality.

I want to believe that my perceived reality is exactly how things actually are. But my experiences tell me that I can be wrong.

I have been involved in three massive enterprise resource planning implementations—SAP, Oracle, and McGladdery. I was personally disappointed with all three outcomes though the problem may have been that I used an unrealistic implementation for each. Data collection and interpretation have severe limitations. Knowing that, though, I would not drive a car without a dashboard in the same way that I would not run a company with an imperfect dashboard. Flying blind and running a company blind both likely lead to disastrous consequences.

The keys are to have the discipline to stay with the process and iterate until we get at least a 10 percent advantage.

In Wilmington, analytics will be a central tool to inform our decision-making. On the pitch, we plan to go the extra distance to ensure the technical staff have high analytics fluency in recruit profiles, pregame scouting reports, postgame team and player reports, and league benchmarks. We will likely add a part-time analyst or agency to help aggregate and interpret the data. Over time, we would like to build our own proprietary data collection with location data as sensor technology advances. There are still large gaps in soccer analytics, but the collection time, processing-speed hardware, and interpretive know-how improve annually.

Analytics will be foundational to our fan-centric experience. We hope our system gets closer and closer to the experience of talking to all of our fans and understanding what they like and dislike in one place. We will develop fan personas so we understand what game day experiences they really value, as well as what happens between games.

Different customers want different experiences; we will offer the bare bones all the way up to the VIP experience. Ticket pricing will reflect the mix. Online ticketing is standard with industry-accepted metrics. Merchandising sales management is fairly straightforward. Sponsorship sales will be a robust CRM, which helps in the conversion of prospects to clients. Our food hall and beer garden will use a mobile ordering system so we understand what type of food our clients want. We will track how popular the food-delivery-to-seat service is.

Not all data has to be just numbers. We will create a closed social network for prospective fans to vote and make comments so we can create a collective and curated experience together. We want real-time user feedback so we know how to improve game experiences in a shorter period of time.

We will likely share our best practices in fan management with other teams so we can develop league benchmarks. We will keep our best practices in soccer analytics to ourselves.

We are clear-eyed about how the systems won't match expectations, but we will stay committed to the process.

Interview

Matteo Campodonico—Villa Riviera
Chiavari, Italy

Matteo has an easy smile and a sense for aesthetics that would not be expected from a founder of a soccer analytics company. In reality, his background, skills, and location do not lend themselves to data collection and analytics at all. Serendipity—and a little luck at the right time—had a major role in starting a successful business. Matteo grew up in a small town outside of Genoa, Italy, where he studied economics at university. He had no entrepreneurial role models, and the region supported mostly bankers and industrialists. By fate or fortune, Matteo had a youth soccer coach who used unorthodox methods for teaching his players. The truth is, while he worked hard in his first jobs, he had no passion for his livelihood. He started a hobby that evolved into Wyscout, one of the most influential companies in the global multibillion-dollar soccer business.

CHRIS: Welcome, Matteo. Tell me how you grew up.

MATTEO: A normal story, really. I grew up in the tourist town of Calgary with 27,000 people, not far from Genoa, Italy. My parents were doctors. I had two sisters and two adopted brothers. My family life greatly influenced my ability to create businesses. It challenged me to consider other people's perspectives and to have an open mind. This upbringing helped me understand how you approach people and how to start a conversation while managing stress.

We always had lots of friends at the house for dinner. We had a big home in a small town; everyone knew each other. That was my life. I am grounded in place. In fact, years later, my parents' house became Wyscout's headquarters. When all my siblings left, my parents lived in a big, empty house. When Wyscout was growing so fast, we needed a big office. I asked my parents if they would please move so we could grow. They were relieved to not have to maintain the big house. It was so comforting to move back home with this new business.

I was classically trained—Greek and Latin—in high school. At the University of Genoa, I studied business and economics. For four years, I had never heard the word *startup*. The career choices were accountant, corporation manager, industry, or finance. No one told me the option to become an entrepreneur.

CHRIS: Did you want to become an entrepreneur when you were in college?

MATTEO: Oh, no. I didn't know what I wanted to do. I wanted to earn income. I was really lucky because I found a great job. A software company hired me to be a business analyst to evaluate the business plans of startups. That's where I met people who were passionate about turning their dreams into companies. After a few years, I wanted to feel the way they did but did not know what to do. I thought about it for years. And then, one night, I woke up with an idea.

When I was seventeen years old, I played lots of soccer. I had a great coach who used to record Series A professional games on VHS. He would show us positioning, runs, and patterns on video clips on a TV. In 1995, no one in Europe was using video analysis. The idea stuck with me. But I could not pursue it as I had two young children and needed a steady paycheck.

I decided to change jobs because I get bored if I do the same routine over and over again. I wanted to be challenged. I took a job at a bank that paid better. I bought a camera and would record amateur games as a hobby on weekends with a friend. Over time, the video analysis business grew. I threw myself into the bank work during the week and the video analysis on the weekends. I was open with my colleagues and boss about my weekend hobby.

CHRIS: How did it go from hobby to legit business?

MATTEO: The growth was not a flash but step by step. We had a $300 camera with a tripod and basic video-editing software on a PC. My cofounder Amato and I would record Sunday morning amateur matches and give DVD samples to coaches. There were 672 teams in our area. Over time, we would reduce games to twenty minutes with chapters on different aspects of the game. Teams started paying us to create the videos. Even more amateur coaches wanted our service, so we hired friends to work on the weekends.

In 2005, I asked my partner Simona if I should reach out to the local professional team in Genoa in Serie A. She said to go for it as the worst they can do is say no. So we recorded a public training session and created a DVD. A few days later, I waited for the head coach to come out of the training facility. I introduced myself and handed him a letter and the DVD. The next day, Genoa's press officer called to tell me that the coach was impressed. They invited us to record the Sunday match. After they saw the match, they invited us in to talk. We were really nervous. When they asked for the service, we gave them a price that we had made up. They accepted, no questions asked!

That was our big break. We worked hard for years only to wait to give a DVD to a head coach in a parking lot on a rainy day.

CHRIS: Amazing! Did you offer any analytics?

MATTEO: No. No. Remember, we are Italians. We wanted videos where we could see the artistry and movement. It's not like the U.S., the UK, and Germany, who like the numbers. In the beginning, we did only video analysis. We were so happy to record Genoa's home games and share the videos.

After a while, Genoa asked if we could record other teams in Serie A and do opposition analysis. We weren't allowed in the other stadiums, so we recorded the games on TV and edited the video with analysis.

The sporting director called us to help them recruit players from South America. We asked for some time to consider it as we did not have access to South American games. There were no YouTube or streaming services at that time. Over a few months, we recruited Italians living in South America through our friends' network. Skype was just launched, so we could afford to develop this network cost effectively. We would pay them a little to record local games on TV and send the video to us. We edited the games and provided analysis. Genoa loved it! We started expanding to more countries around the world with our Italian connections.

By 2006, now that one Serie A team used our service, all teams wanted the video analysis. Professional teams in neighboring countries wanted the service. There were other video analysis providers, but we had the first-mover advantage in professional soccer in Europe. I would visit teams like Roma and Palermo on the weekends and on my days off. It was getting nearly impossible to work at the bank and support the startup's growth. Amato struggled to manage the logistics of teams of people editing the videos on computers and creating DVDs.

One day, my boss called me into his office. He made an offer I could not refuse: Take one year and try to make the startup successful. If it did not work, then forget about the startup and work for the bank. He said it was now impossible to do both.

CHRIS: Wow! That's a really great boss. Would that often happen in Italy? I don't think that happens much in the United States.

MATTEO: It happens in Italy. People are more humanistic here. For years, I worked hard for him. I gave everything to the bank. I think he recognized my efforts. I am so grateful that he let me pursue my dream and gave me a backup to support my family.

CHRIS: In the United States, many startups begin as side hustles that make a bit of money but not enough to make a career change. Help me understand how you recognized the opportunity. When did you know that you needed to do this startup?

MATTEO: By 2007, we had another breakthrough for our business, now called Wyscout. Technology-wise, the YouTube platform, namely videos stored online, had become more stable and crashed less. Second, a really bad day led to a huge trajectory change.

On the last day of the transfer window, I was meeting with the sporting director of Genoa. With a few hours until the deadline, the president called frantically with the news that the owner was willing to invest in buying a particular player. The director and his assistant frantically looked at all the DVDs on his desk and office for the desired player. I tried to help but had no idea where he had put the video. The deadline passed with no offer because the director did not want to commit to a player whose play he could not remember.

In all the yelling and cursing, I thought to myself, why can't we create a video database online of all the players in many countries? The user can access the video with a few taps of their fingers.

CHRIS: Amazing. So, a typical service startup will focus on an anchor client, which is Genoa. You validated the demand for the service with them. You are creating your own product by shooting and editing videos. And then your distribution was visiting the different clubs and sharing the DVDs. How did you convince people to pay you for the analytics and intellectual property? And what was the basis of the brand or the promise?

MATTEO: The truth is that we followed the money. At that point, agents would send their players' highlights on DVD. Italian sporting directors had highlight DVDs everywhere. Our promise was that we could show entire games of when the players touched the ball, the highlights, and the lowlights. They would see the quality of the opposing players and other factors like the quality of the pitch.

There is so much money around the buying and selling of players. We could provide an objective reality of these players, who are the greatest expense to the club. Also, teams could save money by not sending scouts everywhere. They would have a first look at the video. All the clubs understood the value creation. It was like selling candy to kids.

CHRIS: When did you realize this was going to be a real business?

MATTEO: The idea crystallized in 2006. While the business was growing quickly, we needed cash. Italian soccer clubs are notoriously slow in paying bills. A friend introduced an angel investor whose family was in the steel business. I told him my story. He loved that I took a year off from the bank to start a business involved in soccer and video. He also liked that someone wanted to start a business in our small town. After thirty minutes, he said that he would check up on my family. Afterward, he sent the money.

CHRIS: Wow. What did you do with the investment?

MATTEO: We developed an online platform over two years. We thought that it would work well for the Italian market and eventually Spain. I started traveling more and more to other countries to grow the business. In 2010, a large English agency invited me to London. We set up a partnership quickly. The English clubs took interest once the agency shared the product with their players. That was our ticket into the English market. It brought so much credibility. The transfer markets were exploding in value. Our tool was perfect for all that expansion.

CHRIS: In high-growth phases, business is driven by finding the right people. How did you approach that? And how did you figure out what worked and what didn't work?

MATTEO: Honestly, the best employees were the ones who were available immediately and we could afford. On the production side, we looked for friends of friends who we could trust and who worked hard. We could teach them recording and editing. For the sales force, it was difficult as I was limiting sales in that I was the only person selling. I could only call on so many accounts. I needed to find salespeople who already knew sporting directors and coaches. I came to realize those player agents already had these relationships. Agents wanted to earn commissions, especially if their players weren't selling in that transfer window.

Once I made the decision, it was not hard to find player agents all over South America and Europe. They had local knowledge, which helped us go even deeper in the second, third, and fourth divisions of those countries. From 2011 to 2013, we greatly increased our reach and sold access to our video library. While the growth was amazing, the competition was starting to develop around us.

CHRIS: So, in that time, you created a new "product" by providing video of players in South America and Northern and Central Europe. You built out distribution and sales to clubs in these same areas as well. And competitors had caught on to what you were doing and copying you. What happened next?

MATTEO: The growth was crazy. We hired so many new people. We needed to establish a vision and strategy to solve the problems of tomorrow. We started with finding ways to do our operations cheaper and faster. We worked on our branding and marketing to reflect the growing maturity of our business. Finally, we made time to look into what customers were asking for. The more forward-thinking customers wanted us to compile player data based on our videos. They wanted us to do more work for them. A large number of our customers did not initially want data analytics. But we pushed ahead as we made the bet that analytics is the demand of tomorrow.

We already had a team of twenty analysts in Italy. We quickly learned that economics would not work at all. We needed a lower-cost analytical team. By chance, I was friendly with an Italian sports director who lived in Bulgaria. I was so happy when he agreed to run the operation. But then the real work began. We needed to find twenty employees who really knew football. We did not care if they knew about the technology as that could be taught easily. It took time to develop a soccer test and teach that many staff to analyze games quickly. We had to send over servers with games on hard drives as there was no cloud technology available. Over time, the organization developed protocols for marking and tagging videos as well as transcribing them into analytics. That is how we developed video and data analytics with a global reach.

CHRIS: So there's a beginning, middle, and end to everything. Talk a little bit about your decision to sell the business. What was your state of mind?

MATTEO: By this point, Wyscout had a dominant 80 percent market share. We reached a revenue wall of about 30 million euros. I am a creator, not a maintainer. We set out on a goal of being the Bloomberg platform for soccer. The Bloomberg financial platform branched off into news, media, and other services. We were staffed to create the platform, not these new sports. We were an Italian business that was really good at what we started. We could not go into other sports like basketball or American football as there were established players. I knew we needed an external partner or buyer to take the business to the next level.

I also needed a change. Startups are really hard. I was forty-four years old—not twenty-five. My partner and I have five kids. I told her that I thought we could grow the business by 20 percent annually, but to maintain 50 percent growth we would need more capital and external resources. My angel investor agreed. We looked into an IPO. At the same time, we received an offer to buy 100 percent of the business. That was a shocker.

After more thought, we realized that we faced limited growth options with the current path as well as the risk of raising money through an IPO. We negotiated aggressively to keep the headquarters in our hometown. We distributed payouts to the employees as a result of the cash sale. It was one of the hardest decisions I had to make. But I still think it was the right one.

CHRIS: Amazing. Where do you see the growth opportunities in soccer video and analytics?

MATTEO: The truth is that the sport has become digital. Soccer culture has been resisting this change because it is very traditional. The top clubs understand the need for a digital pillar in their organization. Some have adapted to the digital revolution faster than others. Because information can equate to money, less wealthy clubs can compete more easily if they have more information to innovate. You would be surprised at how few clubs fully use both video and data analytics.

I don't see any major breakthroughs in the product. Of course, data collection and cleaning can improve but maybe by only 20 to 30 percent. That is a combination of hardware and software.

The big upside is when the clubs adopt the digital view of reality. There are fewer and fewer coaches who just rely on the eye test. Video and data analytics adoption is growing. But it takes time. The culture needs to change.

CHRIS: So in terms of data collection, there's a little room for improvement. The culture needs to change. Perhaps there are opportunities for data visualization, which will help in the adoption and implementation of normal coaching and workflows. Video and data analytics in recruiting is commonplace, but in coaching, the implementation is uneven.

If you consider business analytics, it is a few years ahead. But they're still all struggling. What do we do with all this data? What is the noise, and what is the signal? I have spoken to various sports organizations. They say, hey, we've got all these really cool data. But, nobody knows how to use it all. And the different departments don't talk to each other at all. So the organizational workflows stay the same as they used to be while the data just grows in storage.

MATTEO: Yes, that is another opportunity, data integration where different departments have access to relevant information and leadership has integrated dashboards, so they know where the ship is sailing. More data is good, but interpretation and action is much better. This will be the next big analytics opportunity.

CHRIS: How about this? I attended a soccer analytics conference recently. Garth Lagerwey, the general manager of the Seattle Sounders, said that sports betting in the United States would accelerate MLS teams into sports analytics. The logic is that as sports bettors and the public get better versed in analytics, it's going to put more pressure on clubs to incorporate analytics. My sense is that the MLS is a little further ahead in terms of analytics adoption. Also, MLS teams will innovate more as they want to close the gap against the better leagues in the world.

MATTEO: I agree. The American soccer culture will adapt more quickly because the general culture accepts analytics more easily.

Moneyball is so American. When the movie was released in Italy, clubs thought to adopt Billy Beane's strategy to analyze the data. No one questions that with baseball it is easier to use analytics while with soccer it is still so hard. In Italy and Spain, the newspapers don't often talk about analytics as much as in the U.S. England is moving more to the U.S. model.

Think about it. The finance industry doesn't buy and sell stocks without data analytics or companies running supply chains. The trend toward analytics is there. Most football clubs need more time to make the adjustment.

CHRIS: What advice would you give to folks who are starting businesses, particularly sports-related businesses?

MATTEO: Just go out there and work. If something makes sense, do more of it. I read Phil Knight's book. He just started going to Japan and buying shoes to sell in the U.S. The only way you can form a perspective is to be working in the space every day. A new idea will not just come out of nowhere. You have to be in the middle of it to see it. I saw my opportunity because I had a coach who used video analysis. The idea came back to me years later when I was bored as a business analyst. I worked in the space, and then doors started to open. It started as a Sunday hobby, and the business has given so much to me, the employees, and the soccer world.

Earlier today, I saw an old friend of mine who, at twenty-three years old, was a waiter. Twenty years later, he is opening his fifteenth bar. He has hundreds of employees. He loves it.

After selling the business, I bought a villa on top of a hill that overlooks my hometown. We are closing on a villa next door with the idea of creating a boutique hotel. For many years, I have spent thousands of nights in hotels of all levels around the world. I have a clear idea of what can be done. I want to celebrate my sense of place and hometown. I want to start something new and make it into something that does not exist.

Sports Betting

Overview

Sports betting represents one of the greatest growth opportunities of our time. The American Gaming Association (AGA) has speculated that the illegal sports betting market is $150 billion—more than fourteen times movie spending—based on a federal government report. Jay L. Zagorsky, an economist at The Ohio State University, estimates the market to be closer to $67 billion based on spending habits in the UK. In comparison, legal sports betting—the Nevada sportsbooks—reaches only $5 billion.

In short, the legal market could grow thirteen to thirty times its current size, depending on which estimate is believed. As a reference, the NFL's total revenue is estimated at $15 billion. The sports betting markets are already much larger than the revenues of the underlying sports. As the segment transitions from illegal local bookies to large online corporations, the ecosystem will grow dramatically. All markets seem to be rising. Nevada's monthly sports betting handle passed the $1 billion mark for the first time ever despite expanded competition from other states.

For most Americans, sports gambling has always been an "illegal" activity, wink, wink. It is so culturally prevalent that the president of the

United States filled out his office bracket on national TV along with an estimated thirty-five million other Americans who submitted their guesses in office pool competitions. Most state legislatures—over thirty-five states—are legalizing sports betting as a "pain-free" way to raise tax revenues. But there is a cost, particularly in gambling addiction. Several studies, some meta, estimate that pathological gamblers represent about 1 percent of the population while gamblers with less serious problems are about 3–4 percent. In these cases, the personal costs are tremendous. The reality is that sports betting—fun and sad—has been intertwined in U.S. culture for some time.

Brief History

Sports betting was taking place in the United States long before the creation of the republic. In the *New York Times*, there is a reference to a Long Island, New York, horse racing track in 1665. Horse racing had its own publications. Three years after the Civil War, the sport was even more organized with the publication of the *American Stud Book*—a journal of the thoroughbreds in the United States. However, during the early 1900s, gambling was outlawed in the time of the temperance movement, whose main focus was to outlaw alcohol consumption. Unsurprisingly, gambling and alcohol became the domain of organized crime. The 1919 Black Sox scandal only encouraged the professional sports leagues to take a stand against gambling.

During the post–World War II boom, sports betting was legalized in Nevada in 1949 to jumpstart tourism. Bugsy Siegel, hit man and trusted associate of mafia boss Charles "Lucky" Luciano, is credited with financing the Flamingo, a casino and hotel. Other mafia families would replicate the business model on the strip by creating other casinos, such as the Thunderbird and Desert Inn. The federal government quickly shut down that effort by imposing a 10 percent tax, which wiped out any potential profits. During that time, organized crime solidified its hold on sports betting through the local distribution of bookies and "enforcement." In 1961, a point-shaving scandal happened at the then-famous Dixie Classic in Raleigh, North Carolina, involving UNC Chapel Hill and North Carolina State basketball players. Apparently, gamblers carrying guns showed up to Reynolds Coliseum wanting their money back from the State players for not honoring the spread agreement. That same year, Attorney General Bobby Kennedy worked with Congress to get a bevy of anti-gambling laws passed in an effort to fight organized crime.

Over time, the Department of Justice deprioritized anti-gambling laws during the 1970s and 1980s. New Jersey citizens voted to legalize gambling in Atlantic City in 1976. Gambling scandals appeared in the 1978–1979 Boston College point-shaving scandal and Pete Rose's MLB ban in 1989.

In 1992, Congress passed the Professional and Amateur Sports Protection Act, which bans states and government entities from legalizing sports betting. Several states, including Nevada, were exempted so they could continue offering sports betting. In 2006, Congress passed the Unlawful Internet Gambling Enforcement Act, which put the onus on financial institutions to block unlawful transactions. Meanwhile, nontraditional casinos, including Native American casinos, started to flourish. The act provided language that would accommodate daily fantasy sports.

By 2009, Delaware and New Jersey had created legislation to legalize sports betting, arguing that gambling laws were a state issue, not the federal government's domain. Supported by a general election ballot, Governor Chris Christie led the charge for the state of New Jersey and the casino operators in Atlantic City. After a couple of unsuccessful efforts, the state of New Jersey petitioned to get the case heard by the Supreme Court.

Fantasy sports developed on a parallel path. In short, participants draft teams from professional sports team rosters and points are awarded based on the players' season-long statistics. In the early 2000s, daily fantasy sports (DFS), or competitions based on one day's games, gained traction.

FanDuel was started in 2009 as its three founders pivoted from news prediction to sports prediction. In December 2010, the company held the first live DFS event in Las Vegas. In 2012, three former VistaPrint employees founded DraftKings to create a one-on-one fantasy baseball competition. In 2013, the segment reached an inflection point when Comcast helped fund FanDuel while Major League Baseball invested in DraftKings to help fund acquisitions of competitors. By 2015, DFS was the leading sports advertiser, which was funded by hundreds of millions of dollars from large private-equity firms. In that year, DraftKings raised funds from

Fox Sports, Wellington Management, and the Kraft Group. In 2016, Draft-Kings and FanDuel attempted to merge, but it was blocked by the Federal Trade Commission as the new entity would control 90 percent of the DFS market. In 2018, FanDuel was acquired by Irish/British betting company Paddy Power Betfair.

According to the Fantasy Sports Trade Association (FSTA), and reported by Ipsos (www.ipsos.com), an estimated sixty million people participate in fantasy sports in the United States and Canada. Over 82 percent of players participate in a season-long league format, 19 percent play daily formats, and 17 percent play both formats. The most popular fantasy sports leagues include baseball, football, hockey, and basketball. Participation in football and baseball are 93 percent and 70 percent, respectively. Total expenditures for fantasy sports are estimated to be $5 billion annually, or about $470 per player, for subscriptions, draft kits, software, and league entrance fees. Much of the entrance fees are paid out in prize money to the players.

According to an ESPN survey, about 8 percent and 1 percent of 18–54-year-old men and women, respectively, play DFS daily. Approximately 14 percent and 3 percent of 18–34-year-old men and women, respectively, play DFS weekly. According to an MLB DFS study by McKinsey & Company, 1.3 percent of players won 91 percent of DFS player profits. On average, the top 11 players paid $2 million in entry fees and each profited $135,000. The top player made $400,000 on $3 million in entry fees. On average, 80 percent of players each lost $25 on entry fees of $49. While the leagues have been reluctant to support sports betting, the leagues have embraced the passion and increased engagement of fantasy sports. DraftK-ings and FanDuel sponsor eighteen and eleven teams, respectively, in the NFL, MLB, NBA, and NHL. MLB is an equity owner in DraftKings.

In May 2018, the Supreme Court ruled in the state of New Jersey's favor, opening a pathway for states to legalize sports betting. By May 2019, sports betting in the state already topped monthly sports betting in Nevada. Other states are scrambling to legalize—and tax—sports betting. Since the legalization, FanDuel has been aggressive in cooperating with existing sportsbooks to create online sports betting on its app. DraftKings has followed suit. The logic is that DFS companies have a trained base of users and can pivot to mobile sports gaming.

In March 2020, the sports betting industry faced a hard stop when Rudy Gobert of the Utah Jazz tested positive for COVID-19. Other professional sports stopped competitions, as did the NCAA. Sportsbooks with physical locations like casinos and retail locations like William Hill suffered the most. Sports bettors mostly stopped betting though there was some action with Taiwanese and Korean baseball as well as Eastern European soccer. Sports betting resumed in July 2020 though betting lines were somewhat distorted by uncertainty in playing lineups.

However, eSports betting flourished during the pandemic as there were few live sports events on which to bet. The global online bookmaker Pinnacle reports that eSports betting is their top category globally. In different competitions, people can bet on competitions between live players or computer simulations. According to the *New York Times*, eSports annual gambling revenue is expected to double to $14 billion. In 2016, Nevada started approving eSports competition betting. State regulators are receiving eSports competition applications almost daily.

Key Players

The key players in eSports are illustrated in figure 2.1.

Bettors

Professional

Serious

Content Providers

Sports

Sports Betting

Sportsbooks

Mobile App

Casino

Leagues

Handicappers

Government

State

Federal

Figure 2.1.
Sports betting.

Bettors

There are three types of bettors: professional, serious, and casual.

PROFESSIONAL

While there are showy exceptions, the professional bettor is likely a low-key personality who loves sports and is looking for a way to make a living. They have a bankroll of $100,000 to $300,000 and make bets of $1–3 million annually, hopefully generating $50,000 to $150,000 annually. Some exceptions make more, but the sportsbooks guard against "sharps" trying to earn money off their clientele. Often, the sportsbooks will limit or cut off bettors who are deemed too successful. As a result, professional bettors will employ surrogates to make bets at sportsbooks to mask their betting. Unfortunately, the bettors and surrogates can get into legal difficulties if taxes are not managed properly.

The demographic skews older, white men, but a new generation of analytics-driven twenty- and thirty-year-olds are entering the segment through DFS. Their greatest pain point is exceeding their bet maximum as sportsbooks want to hedge their bets. Their bet amounts can be limited to $500 to $2,000 per game. Professional gamblers generally survive the longest because they often make small bets on several games. They are grinders. However, sportsbooks remember and limit bettors who take advantage of early, outlier betting lines. Professional gamblers manage their game selection more like conservative fund managers who can't hedge their choices. They are constantly looking for better information and data to give them an edge. Most have built up great informal networks where they share information but still keep the secret sauce to themselves. Several professional bettors appear on sports radio, TV shows, and internet sites as experts as a way to supplement their lifestyle.

SERIOUS

These gamblers tend to skew over thirty-five years old and are middle- to upper-income white men. On average, he wagers more than $1,200 annually. He wants to be known as good at gambling in part because that establishes credibility in other parts of his life. He likely listens to one or two podcasts weekly, checks sports content sites multiple times daily, and may subscribe to one or two handicapper websites. He uses free picks with his favorite handicappers.

Watching sports is an integral part of his family and friends network. His pain point is that he wants an edge and is willing to pay for it. The demand includes new content, handicappers, or websites.

CASUAL

This segment is the holy grail for the gambling industry. These 25–60-year-old male gamblers have bet on March Madness pools. Their gambling gateway was likely small bets in DFS on DraftKings or FanDuel. This group is estimated to be about eight to ten million. However, this number will likely grow dramatically with the legalization of online gambling. He will likely use free handicapper picks and just learn about sports betting resources, including how-to videos on YouTube, content providers, and handicappers. The industry is trying to determine the best way to educate and establish long-term relationships with new gamblers whose number will be many times higher than existing professional and serious gamblers.

Sportsbooks

A sportsbook is a place where a gambler can make a wager. Legal sportsbooks—often casinos—are located in Nevada, Oregon, Montana, and Delaware, although other states are legalizing sports gambling. These domestic sportsbooks have been facing competition from offshore sportsbooks, which are often based in the Caribbean and Central America. Offshore sportsbooks have been operating and innovating for many years. The Unlawful Internet Gambling Enforcement Act does not expressly prohibit Americans from engaging in sports wagering. There are U.S. laws aimed at stopping U.S. bettors located in the country from depositing and withdrawing from offshore sportsbooks. The primary means of control is to require U.S. banks to flag transactions between customers and offshore sportsbooks. These transactions are inconvenient but not illegal. However, offshore sportsbooks often offer a more seamless online betting experience with a wider range of options without the need to physically visit a casino to place a bet. States such as Nevada, Pennsylvania, and New Jersey can now accept bets as long as bettors are physically located in those respective states. The domestic sportsbook mobile-betting experiences have significant room to improve.

Domestic sportsbooks have traditionally offered betting lines so that the betting amounts are split evenly. Lines move in an effort to balance supply and demand. The traditional sportsbook business model is to take a 10 percent commission, called a vig or juice, for facilitating the bet. They generally take bets from all types of gamblers. However, new entrants such as William Hill have reportedly taken the position of limiting the betting of consistently winning gamblers, preferring to deal with smaller, more emotion-driven bettors. While this has caused a significant outcry from traditional bettors, William Hill has utilized this novel business model as it acquires over a hundred physical locations in Nevada with expansion in New Jersey.

Domestic sportsbooks—often the arm of a local casino—have significant lobbying clout that will impact legislation in the states. These casinos have been successful in convincing lawmakers to delay DFS online companies like DraftKings and FanDuel.

Handicappers

These men are at least forty years old and have likely worked at sportsbooks or are professional gamblers. They are looking to supplement their income by offering picks on handicapper websites or making appearances on podcasts and sports radio or TV. Most offer free picks but then charge for access to their predictions—anywhere from $9 daily to $1,250 for a season. Several websites such as covers.com, sportsline.com, and vegasinsider.com aggregate handicappers and content. The websites often share revenue with the handicapper.

Daily Fantasy Sports Companies

DraftKings and FanDuel have over 90 percent of the DFS market. As states legalize sports betting, legislatures are enacting laws to protect local casinos. These measures include a twelve- or eighteeen-month delay to when online-based companies can offer gambling. The battle between DFS and domestic and offshore sportsbooks legislatively and in the marketplace will be a key ecosystem influencer in the coming years.

The Confluence of Sports and Sports Betting Content Providers

There are a multitude of providers: ESPN, Fox Sports, NBC Sports, CBS Sports, Bleacher Report, Barstool Sports, and local newspaper coverage. This segment is very mature in the life cycle. Many of these enterprises are contracting while startups are being acquired by large media companies, such as how Time Warner purchased Bleacher Report in 2012. At this point, the general sports segment has limited entrepreneurial potential with the exception of supporting content moving to virtual reality.

Sports podcasts, such as Bill Simmons, The Herd, and The Totally Football Show, have flourished over the last five years even though income only comes from sharing content with TV or being the market leader in the category. Podcasts for nontraditional sports—U.S. soccer, rugby, and lacrosse—are looking for their audience.

Ten years ago, sports betting content was only available on newsletters and occasionally sports radio. Handicappers—former sportsbook employees and professional gamblers—were the key source of the content. In anticipation of the deregulation of sports betting, Vegas Stats and Information Network (VSIN) was the first mover in a sports betting-focused network. In February 2017, the emerging network was launched by broadcaster Brent Musburger, talent agent Brian Musburger, attorney Todd Musburger, and documentary film producer Dave Berg. Located in the South Point Casino in Las Vegas, VSIN video broadcasts online and on SiriusXM radio. They plan to include broadcasts from New Jersey's Ocean Resort Studio. The network has a video broadcasting distribution with New England Sports Network and offers several podcasts.

Since the Supreme Court decision, traditional media companies have been entering sports betting content. In September 2018, Fox Sports started broadcasting the hour-long show *Lock It In*. ESPN launched *Daily Wager*, a one-hour Monday to Friday show, which uses a similar format as ESPN's other offerings. Time Warner's Bleacher Report has added sports betting content to its 9.5 million consumer base. In early 2019, Bleacher Report announced that it would be building studios inside Caesar's Palace in Las Vegas. USA Today broadcasts sports betting content from the Mandalay Casino in Las Vegas. The initial tremendous enthusiasm has been dampened by modest initial viewership of *Lock It In* and *Daily Wager*. Sports betting content adoption by the mainstream will likely take time.

Leagues

After many years of fighting against sports betting, the leagues' opinions have evolved at different speeds. All leagues are generally in favor of an integrity tax paid by the sports feed suppliers to fight against match fixing. In addition, the leagues generally support federal legislation—rather than state legislation—to ensure uniform treatment across the country. All the major leagues have entered into sports betting agreements with major gaming corporations, which include data feeds, marketing, events, and enhanced sports betting capabilities. Both the league and individual franchises are entering into agreements with either MGM Resorts or Caesars Entertainment Corporation.

In 2014, the NBA was the first major league to break from other leagues and support legalized gambling. As early as 2017, NBA Commissioner Adam Silver felt that "legalized betting is inevitable." In November 2018, the commissioner presented MGM Resorts as the "official gaming partner" of the NBA. Harris Blitzer Sports & Entertainment, the parent company of the Philadelphia 76ers and New Jersey Red Devils, have signed a sports betting agreement with Caesars Entertainment.

The MLB has also resigned itself to the inevitability of legalized gambling. Commissioner Rob Manfred broke from his predecessor Bud Selig with this position. In November 2018, the commissioner named MGM Resorts the "official gaming partner" of the MLB.

The MLS has been generally supportive of legalized gambling, in part because legal gambling on soccer matches is so prevalent in other soccer-playing countries. In March 2019, MLS announced that it was partnering with MGM Resorts in a new soccer betting platform called Roar Digital.

Previously noncommittal on its position, the NHL has stopped short of a federal solution but has advocated for consistency. In October 2018, the commissioner made MGM Resorts the "official gaming partner" of the NHL.

The NFL was the last stalwart against sports betting. By 2017, the league indicated that they were open to in-game wagers. Moreover, the league approved of the Oakland Raiders moving to Las Vegas in 2019. In January 2019, the NFL granted Caesars Entertainment the right to use NFL trademarks within its casino resort properties in both the United States and the UK.

According to the AGA, there were over thirty official partnership agreements between professional leagues/teams and casinos/sportsbooks in 2019. Many states passed legislation for sportsbooks to operate inside professional sports arenas.

Key Factors for Growth

STATE LEGALIZATION

The key driver for growth will be the legalization of gambling. Clearly, the greatest opportunities are in California, New York, Texas, and Florida though there has been strong resistance for various reasons. Surprisingly, smaller states like New Hampshire and Arkansas have quickly followed the first movers, New Jersey and Delaware. The most important—and contentious—considerations include protection of existing casinos, addressing gambling addiction, and how new tax revenues will be used. Moral objections seem to be growing fainter. New legislation is being enacted with growing speed. During spring 2020, COVID-19 caused legislatures to tap the brakes on gambling legalization. As the virus is brought under control, legislatures will likely greatly accelerate approvals as the need for tax income will be very high following the pandemic. With two-thirds of states having approved some form of sports betting, it seems like only a matter of time until other legislatures submit to the temptation of more tax revenues.

ONLINE BETTING

The users want the process to be fast and easy. Sports betting will flourish once wagers can be made easily on mobile devices. Offshore sportsbooks have created great user experiences to overcome the stigma of offshore betting. Currently, bettors have to be physically located in New Jersey or Nevada to place bets. The current mobile solution for domestic sportsbooks has great opportunities to improve. While DFS providers DraftKings and FanDuel have great user experiences, most states require new ventures to wait eighteen to twenty-four months to launch in an effort to protect local casinos. This transition will likely slow U.S. sports betting growth by twelve to eighteen months as domestic sportsbooks iterate their product to standard practices.

CHANGING PERCEPTIONS

Sports betting has entered the mainstream in large part due to March Madness. According to the AGA, approximately forty million Americans submit seventy million NCAA tournament brackets. Fantasy Sports is another bridge. According to the FSTA, 59.3 million people participated in fantasy sports in North America in 2018. Millennials are driving the growth—the average participant age was 32. Perceptions will likely continue to change favorably to sports betting as states legalize the activity and sports content providers integrate betting programming into their core offering. Naturally, any news of game fixing will likely create a temporary public relations setback.

BATTLE BETWEEN DFS AND DOMESTIC AND INTERNATIONAL SPORTSBOOKS

As mentioned earlier, the conflicts between DFS and domestic and offshore sportsbooks will shape the legislative landscape and marketplace. All players appear to be well capitalized. DFS and offshore sportsbooks will likely be aggressive in their expansion into new markets, while domestic sportsbooks will protect their territory as they scale their sports betting. This competition will likely lead to faster innovation in the marketplace though it will likely slow down legislative approvals.

Constraints

CAPITAL A great deal of capital will likely be needed for most startups in sports betting since the incumbents have a large head start and access to capital.

EXPERTISE AND NETWORK Many years of expertise and long-standing networks are needed. More expertise and broad networks can lower capital requirements.

LEGISLATION The major pain point is that sports betting is still illegal in a majority of states. Entrepreneurs do not have the capital or time to lead legislative change. This pain point will ease over time.

UNEDUCATED CONSUMERS Time will be needed to educate consumers. While there are multiple resources on how to gamble on YouTube and online courses, trust is a key sticking point. Enterprises will build a strong business if they can successfully educate the consumers. This education process will require capital to develop.

Opportunities

Barring an extraordinary advantage, there are few to no opportunities in sports content and new sportsbooks due to oversaturation and huge capital requirements. Small, private sportsbooks—really a closed community of sports bettors—are possible with the right connections, sufficient capital, and legal wrangling. A professional sports bettor is a grinding lifestyle that requires a mindset of being content with winning just a little more than losing.

COVID-19 punished the sports betting industry because it was hard to make money if there were no games on which to bet. Those sportsbooks with retail operations or casinos bore the greatest brunt. However, these businesses are generally well capitalized with comparatively low headcounts. While demand has dampened due to the recessionary effects of the virus, the bounceback will likely be immediate as long as college and professional sports are being played. The intermittent nature of the games will likely lead to a more volatile recovery rather than a quick V-shaped comeback.

"INVESTMENTIZATION" OF SPORTS BETTING In three to five years, sports betting management will professionalize much in the same way funds management has in finance. The funds will resemble mutual funds but will likely have an entertainment component as investors will enjoy the narratives as much as making money. In June 2015, Nevada successfully launched entity-based gambling funds. However, the program was put on hold in part because of several bad players and a lack of support from the Securities Exchange Commission (SEC). After sports betting legalization at the state level, this type of funds management will restart as the market gets deeper and general perceptions change. SEC backing will likely lengthen the approval process.

SPORTSBOOK SERVICES Sportsbooks have invested considerably in technology. Large players such as International Gaming Technologies have provided traditional gaming services for years. They will easily transition to sports betting. Opportunities can exist for enhanced mobile user technology. Sportsbooks will always be open to evaluating improved predictive capabilities to ensure proper pricing of initial lines and user performance monitoring.

SPORTS BETTING CONTENT This segment will likely grow as the legalized betting market develops. The traditional sports content providers have moved into this space with an initial muted response. Focused, pay-for-access analysis and content will likely flourish over time. Handicappers will likely professionalize their look and feel on websites and podcasts to garner more subscription fees. Data-driven analytics prediction handicappers will likely emerge with a growing following as betting and analytics go more mainstream.

Personal Startup

I love sports. And I have taken huge bets with my capital and career. But I was never much of a sports bettor. Perhaps it's because, from an early age, I've seen things go really wrong. I have seen things go right for thirty minutes in a state championship game with over four thousand quiet home fans. And then, my left defender slips in the dewy evening grass. I had no chance to make a save as I stood surprised in front of the goal. The crowd erupted and became hostile since we were the visitors. The trend inexplicably changed. By the end of the game, we gave up five goals in one of the most lopsided defeats in soccer state championships. Chaos theory is an attempt to explain systems that are highly sensitive to initial conditions even though they were first thought to be completely random.

In college, I saw a dear friend—who said he could not lose betting on Mets games—end up losing so much that bookies really threatened to break his legs with a bat. He worked over twenty hours extra every week for several years to pay off the bank loan he needed.

But I learned about the world of sports betting through a side door. A friend of mine left me a message to call him back about an interesting opportunity. I had worked with him in health-care innovation, particularly in artificial intelligence and mobile apps. He said that he had met an AI shop that specializes in stock market forecasting and sports betting. My friend set up a meeting to talk about applying AI to a health-care innovation project.

I met with the founder and my friend in some slick offices in a refurbished tobacco warehouse that screamed startup cool. He had a great vibe to him and was super tech savvy. He was also super fit, but his gray hair gave away his age. We clicked as we shared our interests in AI, cycling, and sports in general. I asked him about his AI, but he was coy about how it worked. He showed me a deck of various clients and performance charts. They were impressive given the accuracy of the predictions. I pressed more on the tech. But he stood firm even though I signed an NDA. He said that he had trust issues after a previous partner made off with intellectual property that he developed. Over the course of several hours, I shared my personal history. He talked about his past and his current lifestyle full of grandkids. I was impressed with him—a super tech grandfather.

Over the next several weeks, we got to know each other even more. I did my due diligence. When the CTO abruptly left the company soon after, I called him to ask why. He had positive things to say about the founder but explained that he wanted to go in a different direction. When I asked about the technology, he was in the dark. The server was in a separate room and he had never entered it. I found that strange, but the founder seemed old school.

During a visit, he asked me to join as CEO to scale the business. He generously offered significant equity. I was surprised and ecstatic. I explained my other obligations, but he liked my track record, credibility, and work rate. After some reflection, I concluded that the opportunity was a way for me to quickly learn about AI from the inside with a great deal of ownership. I signed up.

We focused on equity markets and sports betting as the system had the most experience in these areas. Health care would have to wait. A mutual friend set up a meeting with the fund manager for a local university endowment. The fund manager, who managed several university endowments, was as impressed as I was. After asking for more data, he asked us to start a three-month pilot immediately. We did some fundraising presentations with local investors.

When starting the pilot, the AI founder asked if we could accelerate discussions with a successful sports bettor who was very interested in the work in NFL predictions. We took several meetings in Las Vegas with potential investors as well as a former NFL player who had done color commentary on NFL games.

As it was late summer, we decided to start an NFL wagering podcast, which compared predictions from AI, a traditional sports bettor, and an NFL insider. We agreed that this was the best low-cost way to build awareness and eventually create a call to action. While I had done podcasts before, it took time to get the chemistry right. After several weeks, predictions from the professional sports bettor were most accurate, followed by the AI and the NFL insider. The AI founder indicated that he needed to make adjustments. We pressed by asking about the dataset being used. We were stumped by his answer. The algorithm did not use prior plays. It was clear that the system was not machine learning; it was traditional AI in which humans define the rules. We started to figure it out.

As we were more than three-quarters through the season, we held off launching the service until the following year. More states were legalizing sports betting. The NFL and the country were coming out of the pandemic. I wanted to develop more comparables.

By sheer luck, a pro soccer player friend had a master's in statistics while a student of mine had been working with machine-learning platforms on Amazon and IBM Watson. We settled on soccer since we had easier access to that data. For several months, we tested traditional AI and machine learning, watching the platform look for patterns in the data. It was lots of fun to track Premier League results each week. Trends started to emerge.

I learned of other sports betting shops, which ranged from math PhD students doing sports betting for fun to former PhD students who were tight-lipped about their work.

During the NFL playoffs, the AI predictions fell to 45 percent accuracy, well below the acceptable level of 52 percent. It was not working. I received an email from one of the investors we met earlier in the summer. The investor laid out a rambling argument that the AI founder had reworked the data to show that the system correctly predicted the outcomes. In short, he appeared to have cooked the results. Shortly thereafter, I got a call from our mutual friend, who had come to a similar conclusion, even though the AI founder was well-known in the community. I was shocked.

In the office, I confronted the founder. He was extraordinarily defensive when I laid out the details including his initial presentation to me. He claimed that the algorithm was not working properly due to some hardware changes. No progress had been made on the stock market predictions. The most likely explanation was that the algorithm did not work or he was not honest or both. At that point, it was obvious that something was not right.

As for the collaboration with the NFL podcast, the sports bettor, and the NFL insider, we did not have a viable AI predictor because my work with traditional AI and machine learning did not get close to the 57 percent accuracy target. We decided to wind down the podcast project.

What do I conclude? The first takeaway has nothing to do with sports betting. Be careful who you choose as a partner. If it seems too good to be true, then it probably is. After this experience, it is easier to understand how a Bernie Madoff Ponzi scheme could grow so well, knowing how folks in the community vouched for the guy.

Sports betting has a seedy history given that the pastime was illegal in most states until recently. Like finance, the big players—FanDuel, DraftKings, MGM Resorts, and others—will dominate the landscape by vacuuming up any innovative ideas using the capital they possess. Sports AI specialty shops will get bought up. They will have to change their algorithms in real time to keep up. The big players will make their high margins on smaller, more emotionally driven bettors. They will cut off larger analytical bettors who establish a successful track record.

Fundamentally, random factors greatly influence games. Most systems can't beat the 52 percent success rate over time. I personally don't like those odds even though I think I am well informed. But my track record was not much better over time.

I do think that sports prediction using machine learning will have some promise as we improve data collection, particularly in location and body position. But competition will likely be fierce until proprietary databases become more popular. Sports wagering media will be a great challenge as traditional sports media will add more wagering programs.

As sports betting is still not legal in my state, I will take a wait-and-see approach while learning more about technology and developing the network.

Interview

Ken Murphy—Professional Sports Bettor

I really didn't know what to expect from meeting a professional sports bettor. I had this image of a hairy, heavyset man wearing lots of gold jewelry who smoked cigars and spoke his strong opinions in a South Jersey accent. Ken was far from that stereotype. With a head of white hair and a matching beard, he speaks only after thinking first. His mild Texas accent almost hides his high intellect. The twang creates a gentle juxtaposition between country and analytics when he discusses portfolio management styles and probabilistic-outcome sports betting approaches. When talking to him, there is a distinct sense of mystery—namely, what is not said. He sounds like a patient fund manager when he explains the ins and outs of sports betting.

I was first struck by the thin margins of success in the sports betting business. Ken explained that a successful sports bettor wins 52–58 percent of bets over the long term. Below 52 percent, you lose money. The truth is that sports bettors win a little more than they lose. This means taking lots of small bets rather than having a feeling and betting the ranch.

The professional sports betting life can be a grind because of the tremendous amounts of needed research, positions taken, and money won or lost in each short learning cycle. You really have to love sports to get through the grind. He seems at peace with regularly losing money in a bad streak while not getting cocky when he is on a roll. I marvel how he is okay when he does all the right things but loses due to a ball bouncing the wrong way. I really found some golden nuggets in our conversation on his starting several businesses in sports betting.

CHRIS: Ken, tell me about how you grew up and got into sports betting.

KEN: Well, we have to go back a pretty long, long way. My father worked for the U.S. government in the 1960s and 1970s. I lived much of my childhood in Latin America and returned to the U.S. for college. I played sports at various levels. I have always had a passion for sports. After graduating, I was very interested in sports betting. In those days, sports betting was fairly primitive. You didn't have computers to gather data and crunch numbers. You worked off data that you pieced together from newspapers. With my analytical background, I found both joy and great success. As a result, I got cut off in several places where they wouldn't take my bets. That was a good lesson. I learned that it is important to keep a low profile.

Over the next twenty years, I got married, started raising kids, and put sports betting aside. I ended up starting several successful small businesses. We just did what sports-oriented families do and played sports. I played a lot of adult softball and coached all the various sports with the kids.

In the late aughts (2008–2010), a friend of mine was living in Las Vegas. He was betting on baseball and asked for my help. I said that it had been a very long time and maybe I could help. At that time, I brought myself into the twenty-first century with all the data. It was much easier to do what I had manually done twenty years ago.

CHRIS: What was the first bet that you placed?

KEN: I can't even remember what I had for lunch yesterday. It was probably maybe a little before 2010. But initially, I was only helping him. And then he said, Ken, this is amazing. You've completely flipped the results for me. You should go into the business of providing your selections for people. I didn't really want to do that. He then suggested that we take a year to work hypothetically with a balance of $200,000. We will identify four or five people who I can provide my selections to free of charge so that we have third-party corroboration of the selections.

After the first year, I made a return of 111 percent. I thought I might be onto something. I lived in Texas at the time, so I wasn't sports betting myself. I was just doing the homework and providing information. About five years ago, the state of Nevada legalized sports entity wagering funds. These Nevada entities could be managed by a licensed funds manager who could accept money from all over the United States. I was the first and the largest sports entity fund. Unfortunately, disagreements between the state and the SEC as well as some unscrupulous fund managers led to the discontinuation of the state program. As a result, I shifted to providing a subscription service for my daily selections.

CHRIS: What are some of the challenges in developing a subscription business?

KEN: Many of the challenges have nothing to do with actual sports handicapping. As I live in Las Vegas, it's completely legal for me to make a sports bet using multiple accounts. I'm already doing the research. Many friends have suggested that I should provide selections to others, but it wasn't something that I really wanted. But the industry has really taken off as sports betting is legalized state by state. We had a pause during the early part of the pandemic, but the growth has resumed in this crazy time.

States that allow mobile betting with reasonable taxes will flourish. New Jersey betting amounts have already exceeded Nevada for some time. There are now over 150 million people who live in states where it is legal to make a sports bet.

Most people are looking at sports betting for the very first time. They're not experts or big bettors. They are looking to get educated by learning the terminology. It's intimidating. What is a parlay or teaser? What is sharp money? My effort is to educate people and allow people to get my insights daily. I think we will be very successful in that endeavor.

CHRIS: How has the handicapping business been different from the funds management you did before?

KEN: The handicapping itself is the same whether you were handicapping for an investment fund when that was legal in the state of Nevada or whether you're handicapping for yourself. Now I'm handicapping for myself as well as a subscription base. In the funds management business, I would bet more money on fewer games. The confidence thresholds were higher. For handicapping, my clients want more bets, so I provide them with all the caveats. I include what I call "checkmark" games, which are games that I like, but for some reason, they don't quite qualify as a game that I would make a substantial investment on.

I feel like everyone who has an investment portfolio should have some sports betting to diversify risk. For those states with legalized betting, these investments have a different risk/reward profile than stocks and bonds. In sports betting, we don't have election risk, climate change, and international relations to worry about. At least, we don't yet.

The truth is that sports betting is not a get-rich-quick endeavor. Most people who take this approach generally end up with a get-poor-quick proposition. The key is to be prudent on how much you bet per game, do the research, and develop an investment philosophy.

CHRIS: I'm really struck by your perspective. You sound more like a fund portfolio manager than a stereotypical sports bettor. You're taking bets within your limits. It sounds like you have a fairly disciplined approach to sports betting. I hear elements of analytics and in collecting data, but at the end of the day, you're trusting your gut.

KEN: Let's be clear. The process needs to be data-driven to be successful in this business. You have to have access to good data, whether you create it yourself or you find a provider. You must have access to good data and be disciplined in the long term. There will be ups and downs with losing days or losing weeks. Last year, I had two losing months—you can go through an extended period. I've gone through five. If you're the type who says I'm going to double up to catch up, then really bad things can happen.

I normally play 1 percent of my available assets allocated to sports betting at any given time. In other words, if I have $10,000 set aside to bet on sports, I would recommend that, on average, you play about $100 a game. There may be once or twice a month when you play $200 or 2 percent, but that would be the max if you want to be a success in the long term. Sports betting is largely a scientific endeavor, but it's part science and part art. The art part is where somebody like me can bring many years of experience and knowledge along with the homework. Often, I make decisions in the final analysis based on subtle pieces of information that most people would overlook. But that means you leave a lot of money on the table sometimes. I prefer to build a consistent long-term data-driven program with a subjective lens.

CHRIS: It sounds like you've gotten into the handicapping subscription business largely because you're already doing the research. It's a nice little add-on as it doesn't require a great deal of additional time. What are some other growth areas? Do you see any prospects in, say, sports betting content? Where are the spaces you think that there's wiggle room for entrepreneurs?

KEN: That's a great question. It goes to the heart of what you're doing with your book. There are so many things happening in the world of sports. Artificial intelligence applications and sports betting are still misunderstood, but it's on people's radar. Three years ago, I never saw a podcast related to sports. Now, everybody's got a podcast; some of them have big followings.

Sports betting entity funds will come back. I will be ready as I have already been through the process of a legal sports betting fund. You'll see Google or Microsoft set up a sports betting exchange. Funds will be created not only in the United States but around the world. I imagine that it will look like Wall Street. Within the next three to five years, large institutional fund managers will make bets on these large global exchanges. Investors will want a return, and the sports betting market is very inefficient now. In short, the market will consolidate to peer-to-peer betting meets the global stock exchange with some third-party validation.

CHRIS: How will sportsbooks be able to survive?

KEN: It will be a segmented market with institutional investors who aggregate money and individual investors who make their own bets. It's not too different from the current stock market. I think the sportsbooks will continue to serve individual bettors.

The current anti-gambling laws are helping perpetuate illegal offshore and onshore betting. Las Vegas is doing just fine even though the New Jersey sportsbooks are building their business. The East Coast sportsbooks are taking business away from illegal betting while governments get additional tax income.

CHRIS: How will COVID-19 impact sports betting in the long run? What are some surprises you've seen from the pandemic?

KEN: One of the biggest surprises is the added uncertainty. You were taking a huge risk betting on games early in the week. Before, a bettor could arbitrage the line earlier in the week versus lines later. But, it's not a great idea to place bets early because a key player could miss the game due to COVID-19. I waited twenty-four hours before a game before I bet, and, in some cases, a game that I liked on Tuesday may be a hard pass on Saturday because the number now is less advantageous. Now, bettors have gotten into the habit of betting at the last minute to wait for any new information. This behavior makes it harder for sportsbooks to balance the bets as the bets come in later.

The trend that has grown tremendously is making bets on smartphones. The pandemic trained people to bet in the comfort of their homes as opposed to going to the casinos. I would not be surprised if we look back and see 2020 as the year when sports betting shifted to majority mobile versus a physical location.

Another huge trend is the growth of eSports betting. We saw first glimpses during the pandemic of virtual NASCAR betting where drivers were sitting in machines racing cars. FIFA 20 soccer game betting hasn't gotten a lot of traction, but it will grow. In the betting segment, there are many people who believe eSports wagering will exceed traditional sports wagering in a few years. The younger generation is going to drive that trend. In Las Vegas, developers are building some palatial eSports venues for high-profile competitions. The television contracts are coming soon. It's regaining steam again. But that's an explosive opportunity.

As for traditional sports, there will be some rule changes that happen to make the game more exciting. These include more MLB teams in the playoffs, adoption of the designated hitter for both AL and NL, seven-inning double headers, or starting extra innings with a runner on second base. There are some purists that don't like the ideas, but I'm somewhat of a baseball purist, and I love it.

Now is the opportunity to experiment and see what works. The truth is that the competition for people's leisure time is so ultracompetitive. Fans watching a fifteen-inning game may not be realistic.

In-game wagering is going to grow dramatically as it's more stimulating when outcomes happen faster. It's not my cup of tea, but young bettors are going to drive the growth. They grew up with video games and social media with immediate gratification. And that may be the saving grace of baseball.

CHRIS: What advice would you give a young entrepreneur who wants to get into the sports betting space?

KEN: Find a segment of the business that interests you. Work in the space for little or no money in order to get a handle on that opportunity if you can afford it. For example, there is a shortage of sportsbook managers and analysts in casinos in newly legalized states.

You can create your own podcast to build a following. There is a lot of garbage in podcasts now, but the cream will rise to the top. Develop expertise in a particular sport; there are always people who look for an edge. The internet has been the great leveler of information on sports. Focus on the niches, such as the obscure games or new eSports where people don't have much intel and the bettors are mostly nonobjective super fans. Do your research and learn from your mistakes. Develop a system over time.

Believe it or not, some of the worst handicappers in the world are former athletes. If you really pay attention to what they say on ESPN or Fox, all the so-called credible pundits are wrong more than half the time. We are at the beginning of a major revolution in sports betting. The opportunities are out there for those willing to put in the work.

If you are really good at a particular sport, then get in touch with me. I'll pay you to help me handicap whatever sport that is. I am always learning . . .

3

eSports

Overview

Behind sports betting, eSports will likely be the second-largest growth opportunity in sports during the next three years. Post COVID-19, the global video game market exceeded $180 billion, more than four times greater than box office revenues and three times greater than music industry sales. Sales from Asia-Pacific and North America represent about 50 and 25 percent, respectively. The growth of individual companies ranges from 30 to 80 percent.

eSports is a segment of gaming that is described as organized, multiplayer video game competitions. Teams are formed, which, if successful, lead to sponsorship to pay salaries and housing costs. The competitions started out as virtual competitions but have evolved into in-person competitions with specially built stadiums. Going forward, phigital—physical and digital—will be the dominant business model in eSports. The U.S. $30 million 2019 Fortnite World Cup was watched by nineteen thousand people at Arthur Ashe Stadium in New York and had 2.3 million concurrent views across Twitch and YouTube. The pandemic paused nearly all eSports competitions from March 2020 into 2022. The Fortnite World Cup was canceled in 2020 and 2021, with Epic Games announcing the competitions would resume in late 2022 and beyond. As with gaming in general, the Asia-Pacific market leads in terms of players and events held.

Revenues for eSports—advertising, broadcasting, and sponsorship—were about $2 billion in 2022. While there is a legitimate debate on whether eSports is indeed a sport, the International Olympic Committee is considering eSports as a demonstration sport in the 2024 Paris Summer Olympics. The 2022 Asian Games have already included eSports as a medal sport when the event takes place in fall 2023. Sponsors—whose money is the lifeblood of sport and entertainment—are certainly taking notice. The 2018 World Championship Finals for the eSports game *League of Legends* had 99.6 million unique online viewers versus 98.2 million TV viewers for the 2019 Super Bowl.

In 2018, technology consultancy Activate was the first to made bold eSports predictions: U.S. eSports viewers were more than 63 million, less than the NFL (139 million) and MLB (83 million) but the same as the NBA (63 million) and considerably more than the NHL (32 million) and MLS (13 million). The pro leagues are looking to take advantage of the new medium. Back then, NBA launched the NBA 2K League, the first mover of U.S. pro leagues to create an eSports league of its own. The games will be televised on Twitch, an Amazon game-viewing platform, which is the thirtieth-largest website by traffic, with fifteen million visitors daily. The NFL has teamed up with EA Sports and the CW network to televise the Madden NFL 19 Championship Series.

Goldman Sachs expects eSports viewers to exceed three hundred million by the end of 2022, comparable to the NFL viewership today, and expects total eSports monetization will reach $3 billion. Prize money is driving growth. For example, in 2019, Epic Games created a $100 million prize pool for the first year of Fortnite eSports tournaments, comparable to the entire eSports prize pool in 2017. Sponsors and advertisers are flocking to eSports as the young, affluent male is turning away from traditional entertainment and is increasingly harder to target.

During the coming years, there will be a redefinition of the athlete. Professional eSports leagues are developing around the world, and a crossover into mainstream sports is in the making.

American universities are already starting to offer scholarships in eSports. According to *Wired* magazine, eSports became a $906 million industry in 2017. Approximately two hundred U.S. colleges offer around $15 million annually in scholarships while university teams compete for millions in tournament prizes. According to the National Association of Collegiate Esports, the average eSports scholarship student obtains $4,800 in annual tuition awards, while others can receive up to half of their tuition.

It is fair to argue whether eSports is defined as a sport in a traditional sense of physical activity, skill, and chance. The reality is that eSports is and will continue to be a greater influence on youth and adult sports. The dramatic growth will create great opportunities for entrepreneurs.

In summary, its $2 billion in revenue is a tiny part of the $300 billion gaming industry but attracts a huge viewership. eSports will experience rapid growth as it provides entertainment and marketing opportunities and a phigital community.

Brief History

eSports has developed in tandem with the computer itself. In 1952, Alexander Shafto Douglas did his PhD work at Cambridge on the interaction between humans and computers using the game *OXO*, a computerized version of tic-tac-toe. Shortly thereafter, in 1958, *Tennis for Two* was created, featuring an early iteration of the joystick. In 1962, Steve Russell, Martin Graetz, and Wayne Wiitanen created *Spacewar!* at MIT using a PDP-1 computer. Fighting against the constraints of a gravitational field and limited fuel and ammunition, the players' spaceships would battle each other. A decade later, in 1972, twenty-four players gathered to compete in the Intergalactic Spacewar Olympics tournament hosted at the Laboratory for Artificial Intelligence at Stanford University. The victor received a year's subscription to *Rolling Stone* magazine.

During the 1970s, video arcades swept the nation with games such as *Sea Wolf!*, *Asteroids*, *Starfire*, and *Space Invaders*. These games included the highest-score leaderboard, which allowed for competition. In 1980, over ten thousand gamers competed at the Space Invaders Championships. William Salvador Heineman was immortalized as the first winner of a national video game competition.

Walter Day, a video arcade owner in Ottumwa, Iowa, founded the Twin Galaxies National Scoreboard, the first video game referee service. He later created *Twin Galaxies' Official Video Game & Pinball Book of World Records* to establish records and rules designed to prevent cheating. In 1983, Day created the U.S. National Video Team, the first known professional gamer team. He developed the North American Video Game Challenge, the first U.S. video game masters tournament.

Japanese game maker Nintendo moved front and center in the early 1990s. They hosted the Nintendo World Championships in thirty U.S. cities starting in 1990. Competitions included *Super Mario Bros.*, *Rad Racer*, and *Tetris*. Not to be outdone, Blockbuster Video and *American GamePro* magazine organized a world video players championship in 1994. Competitors played *Virtua Racing* and *Sonic the Hedgehog 3* on the Super Nintendo and Sega Mega Drive.

In the 1990s, it became clear that the future of competitive gaming would be found in personal computers and networks. As hardware became more and more affordable and powerful, PCs became more available for private households and thus also for the gaming industry. In the mid-1990s, the first big LAN parties allowed gamers to compete with each other. On a small scale, however, gaming over the network exerted an ever-increasing fascination. More and more gamers met at small network sessions and gambled on their favorite games.

A pioneer eSports game, *Counter-Strike*, was launched in a Windows version in 1999. The game was one of the first objective-based multiplayer first-person shooter formats. *Counter-Strike* is now a series with four titles and three spinoffs and is a key game in eSports competitions today. During the last twenty years, eSports have flourished in Korea, the Philippines, and Germany. Staple eSports games include *World of Warcraft* (2004), *League of Legends* (2009), *Defence of the Ancients* (commonly known as *DotA*) (2013), *Overwatch* (2016), *PlayerUnknown's Battlegrounds* (2017), and *Fortnite* (2017).

During the pandemic, all in-person events were put on hold, which has put considerable strain on leagues and teams who count on prize money and sponsorships associated with in-person events. Some leagues are owned by gaming companies, while some leagues and competitions are owned by third parties who are struggling. The workaround is seeking COVID-related support from the super-flush game creators. In addition, teams have fan tournaments where they play games with the fans to generate tournament income for themselves.

The other workaround is returning to remote competitions, but they are tricky due to time zone differences, inherent latency (speed of internet), accusations of direct denial-of-service attacks (to slow latency), and accusations of using aimbotting—a computer program to autocorrect shooter aim and view through walls. Integrity will be difficult to maintain as there are often human monitors at in-person events. Match fixing is also a challenge as prize money escalates while team salaries remain very modest.

As we enter a diminished COVID phase, in person eSports competitions have been scheduled for late 2023 and beyond. Other trends will drive growth.

Because of the pandemic, there has been a greater crossover between in-person sports and eSports. Leagues like the NBA, USL, La Liga, NASCAR, and Formula One have organized events where their athletes play games with professional eSports players. NASCAR hosted the iRacing Series, which attracted a peak of 1.3 million viewers. Time will tell if the industry is negatively affected by disrupted hardware manufacturing or reduced coding productivity due to remote work. COVID-19 appears to be accelerating the trend toward more mobile gaming, which is easy to distribute. The free download with in-game purchase model is becoming the de facto business model. In 2020, Activision Blizzard reported earnings 50 percent above analysts' expectations due to revenues from its mobile edition of *Call of Duty*.

Competition viewership is growing as fans are staying home more. Fans watching events on Twitch doubled during the pandemic. The platform, owned by Amazon, has grown to 1.6 billion hours watched each month. The hope is that eSports will cross over to the mainstream as its athletes make seven figures, viewership increases for both in-person and virtual, and prize money reaches into the millions. Forecasters are cautious about the magnitude of growth as we reach a diminished COVID-19 phase.

Key Players

The key players in eSports are illustrated in figure 3.1.

User

eSports viewers are typically affluent men with an average age of twenty-five. According to the audience research company GWI, the group is 65 to 70 percent

Figure 3.1.
eSports ecosystem.

male, and 73 percent self-report as either middle or higher income. Approximately 73 percent are between the ages of sixteen to thirty-four. Among men sixteen to twenty-four years old, eSports engagement is much bigger in Asia: Philippines (40 percent), China (39 percent), Malaysia (37 percent), Singapore (35 percent), Vietnam (35 percent), and South Korea (31 percent). The United States has a considerably lower amount with only 21 percent, with Europe skewing close though there are exceptions. It has been reported that nine out of ten eSports fans delete cookies, block ads, or use private browsers, making them a difficult segment in which to market. For these reasons, this segment is highly attractive to high-tech and consumer products advertisers and sponsors.

Platforms

Platforms include both livestream and recordings of eSports competitions, personal streams of individual players, and gaming-related talk shows.

TWITCH

Twitch is the eight-hundred-pound gorilla of eSports streaming platforms, with an average of eight million daily broadcasters. With 2.6 million concurrent viewers, Twitch is ranked thirty-third in the world in terms of viewership, outstripping viewers at MSNBC (885,000) and CNN (783,000). On average, Twitch users watch ninety-five minutes daily. In 2014, Amazon bought Twitch for a little less than a billion dollars in part because Twitch traffic was behind only Apple, Netflix, and Google that year.

In 2018, Twitch signed a two-year, $90 million contract to exclusively broadcast the Overwatch League matches. While this figure is modest compared to the $3 billion NFL and $2.7 billion NBA contracts, the Overwatch League annual figure of $45 million is already half the size of the $90 million MLS annual TV contract. Twitch has yet to sign any new eSports contracts in the diminished COVID-19 phase.

YOUTUBE GAMING

YouTube Gaming is a distant second compared to Twitch. Its quarterly concurrent views of approximately 300,000 represent about 25 percent of Twitch's views. YouTube does not break out its gaming views even though two of its top five channels are gaming related. Seventy-four percent of YouTube gamers self-report that they watch videos primarily to improve their gaming skills. YouTube Gaming has entered into the broadcast business with an exclusive relationship with FACEIT's Esports Championship Series and is the unofficial home of mobile eSports titles, including *Clash Royale*.

OTHER U.S. PROVIDERS

In 2016, Microsoft entered the eSports streaming business with their high-performance, low-latency Mixer; the Mixer NYC Studio hosted exclusive eSports and gaming events. In late 2018, Facebook launched the streaming platform fb.gg, which curates live eSports content by analyzing a user's Liked Pages and Groups. Facebook Gaming livestreams events on users' newsfeeds. They have been aggressive in acquiring exclusive broadcasts. Steam TV is a notable mention in that it was launched by the game developer Valve, which has two mega game titles, *DotA 2* and *Counter-Strike*. It will be interesting to see if game developers move downstream to have integrated livestreaming platforms.

CHINESE PROVIDERS

Known as the Twitch of China, Douyu TV has 92 million users and exclusive Chinese broadcasting rights to World Electronic Sports Games and Riot Games's 2018 League of Legends Korea Champions. Huya is also actively involved in eSports along with general-interest livestreaming. Panda TV, ZhanQi TV, and Netease CC are other players looking to take market share in China's burgeoning growth.

Game Publishers

There are a large number of game publishers with remarkable histories. During the last twenty-five years, the industry and ecosystem have evolved rapidly. Let's highlight the largest players impacting the industry.

VALVE CORPORATION

Founded in 1996 by two former Microsoft employees, Valve is one of the most successful publishers; its megahit franchises include *Counter-Strike* and *DotA*. The privately held game producer manages Steam, a gaming distribution platform that sells its own and third-party titles, and Steam TV, a livestream distribution platform. The company is uniquely integrated with production, distribution, and livestreaming.

RIOT GAMES

Founded in 2006 by two USC college roommates, Riot Games is the creator of the megahit *League of Legends (LoL)*. The multiplayer game blew up surprisingly fast given its steep learning curve and competitive nature. The company constantly updates content to satisfy its 100+ million users. In 2011, Riot Games started organizing the LoL World Championships and LoL Championship Series. That same year, the Chinese internet media company Tencent acquired a majority interest in Riot Games. As a result, the company has broad support distribution in China and Asia in general. In addition, offshore sportsbooks provide betting options on the tournaments.

ACTIVISION BLIZZARD

Founded in 1991, Blizzard Entertainment created multiple franchises, including *Overwatch*, *World of Warcraft*, *Heroes of the Storm*, and *Hearthstone*. Activision, a subsidiary, developed the popular *Call of Duty* franchise. The company launched Battle.net 2.0 to track achievements and develop a community across users of their games. Most importantly, they have launched the Overwatch League.

In early 2022, Microsoft announced it was purchasing Activision Blizzard. Regulatory approval has been slow given the combination of the enormous popular *Call of Duty* and Xbox platform. This transaction could represent a game changer as one company will own both a popular game and platform.

EPIC GAMES

Founded in 1991, Epic Games was originally known as the developer for Unreal Engine, a software development platform for developing games and the popular game *Gears of War*. In 2012, the Chinese internet conglomerate Tencent acquired about 40 percent ownership for $330 million. These funds help upgrade Unreal Engine and develop new games. In 2017, the company released *PlayerUnknown's Battlegrounds*, a popular battle royale game and a precursor to its greatest success. The Cary, North Carolina, company launched the free-to-play *Fortnite Battle Royale* in September 2017. By May 2018, the user base had grown to 125 million, and now it exceeds 400 million. In 2018, Epic Games raised $1.25 billion at a $15 billion valuation for acquisitions, supporting startups using Unreal Engine, and $100 million in prize money for a new Fortnite league.

Teams

eSports teams can have multiple squads of up to sixty players who specialize in particular games. The larger teams have managers who recruit and manage players as well as secure sponsorships. In the past, teams would have lots of turnover and often fold. However, successful team management has professionalized with ownership moving to corporations, venture capitalists, and sports team owners from other sports. In the Overwatch League, compensation structures include prize shares, lodging, and health care. Of the top ten teams, several are based in the United States, Europe, South Korea, Russia, and China. Teams have sponsorships from brands like Red Bull and SK Telecom. Prize-leading teams include Team Liquid, Evil Geniuses, Team OG, Newbee, and Fnatic.

Top team players can earn up to $3 million and have up to four million followers. Ninja (Tyler Blevins), the most successful athlete, has eleven million followers. According to CNBC, Blevins self-reported that he makes $500,000 monthly through subscriptions from his Twitch and YouTube broadcasts. Team members often live in the same house and train over fifty to sixty hours a week. Many pro players start in their teens and retire by their mid-twenties due to the lifestyle and burnout.

Sponsors

Sponsorship has grown dramatically as the number of viewers has sky-rocketed. Mainstream companies such as Intel, Red Bull, Mercedes, Coca-Cola, McDonald's, and Gillette see this as an attractive way of appealing to middle- to upper-income 16–35-year-old men.

Tournaments and Leagues

The number of tournaments has flourished in recent years. The largest is organized by game developers with huge purses who treat these events as marketing. A tournament's sustainability is largely determined by local and global sponsors. Tournaments can last anywhere from one day to ten months, including prequalifiers. The largest tournament is Epic Games Fortnite World Cup, with a $100 million purse, equivalent to the total eSports payout in 2018. The sixteen-year-old solo winner won $3 million in prize money in 2019.

Riot Games organizes the League of Legends World Championship. Valve Corporation oversees the International, a massive *DotA 2* tournament, and the Intel Extreme Masters for its *Counter-Strike* franchise. Activision Blizzard organizes the Call of Duty World League and Overwatch League. The latter is organized like a professional sports league with twenty permanent teams in cities throughout the world. Franchise fees are reported to be $20 million to join. Franchise owners include Robert Kraft (Boston Uprising) and Stan Kroenke (Los Angeles Gladiators), as well as several owners who also have NHL franchises. Time will tell if eSports goes the way of permanent teams like the U.S. pro sports model or remains like the European football model of promotion and relegation.

eSports High School and College Teams

At least seventeen states include eSports as a varsity sport, with New York and New Jersey considering joining. PlayVS, a high school eSports league organizer, has raised $46 million from investors like Diddy and Adidas. Though it is in its early days, college scholarships are growing dramatically. Over 175 U.S. colleges award around $15 million in annual eSports scholarships, about $4,800 per person, to compete in tournament prizes. With potential tournament winnings and college scholarships available, it's not hard to imagine that a youth pipeline will develop quickly.

eSports Betting

This area appears to be emerging rapidly from a small base. eSports betting is broken down into "skins" betting and money betting. "Skins" are in-game items that can change the appearance of a player in a game, such as a weapon or clothing. Skins are a virtual currency with low stakes, low barriers to entry, and low friction. Valve's *Counterstrike: Global Offensive* and *DotA 2* were big facilitators to the skins movement as players earned them for performance. Through Steam (Valve's marketplace), new websites sprung up to support the trading and purchasing of skins. Furthermore, specific skins betting platforms were created so bettors will bet skins on a certain professional player winning.

According to research for Narus Advisors and Eilers & Krejcik Gaming, skins betting is by far the most popular, with a handle across all skins betting sites of over $7 billion in 2016 prior to Valve's crackdown. The company, along with several betting websites, was sued by a player for operating gambling sites. However, skins betting remains popular.

eSports money gambling appears to be fairly modest though the large offshore sportsbooks do offer betting lines. The latest estimate is that eSports handled $650 million in 2016. eSports money gambling will face an uncertain growth pattern as general sports gambling will grow dramatically. The challenges include the unclear support of game developers and the lack of data.

Constraints

PARENTS THINK PLAYING VIDEO GAMES IS A WASTE OF TIME Parents worry about their kids' lack of physical activity and the sheer time requirements involved. Most competitive eSports players practice four to eight hours daily while reporting little to no physical exercise. Though it's too early to make conclusions, the prime gaming years are fourteen to twenty-five, based on recent tournament winners. These perceptions will likely slow adoption rates.

GAME DEVELOPERS NOT SHARING DATA Because eSports is all digital, there are enormous amounts of data that can be analyzed. However, the developers and their key stakeholders are largely keeping the data to themselves. In traditional sports, video analysis is often used to capture key data of two to twenty-two players. In eSports, there can be a hundred players whose actions may not be shared on the public video. Oddly enough, insufficient access to data will likely hold back eSports analytics and betting.

CHANGE IN RULES Developers regularly update their games to include new features or character changes. This element is another holdback for eSports analytics and betting.

DEVELOPING GAMES COSTS MORE WITH GROWING EXPECTATIONS With the launch of amazingly complex games like *Fortnite*, consumer expectations are high. The range for a new title can be $10,000 to $250 million (think *Grand Theft Auto*), with top titles regularly reaching $50 million. Top mobile games can range from $10 billion to $20 million. Game complexity drives development costs while marketing costs go up to build awareness in an increasingly noisy marketplace.

Opportunities

This segment will experience tremendous growth for the large game producers, mobile phone networks, team owners, and property developers with lots of capital to create in-person stadiums. eSports is still fairly small in size, with $1 billion in revenues. Imagine that eSports teams will evolve much like traditional sports like youth club, college, minor league, and major league professional teams. However, there are many opportunities for entrepreneurs to look in the seams of the segment rather than the main sections.

LOCAL YOUTH ESPORTS CLUBS Like traditional sports, clubs and leagues will likely flourish in the coming years. It's not too hard to imagine a youth club infrastructure that starts with tryouts on the local level, national youth competitions, and development academies like the U.S. Soccer Federation. Naturally, there will be resistance by parents, but over time the allure will be too strong for the kids.

PRIVATE TRAINING As in traditional sports, the eSports coaching profession will develop. Online curriculums will be created with personal training programs.

DATA COLLECTION AND ANALYTICS Depending on game developers' wishes and levels of cooperation, eSports data collection from third parties will take place through video analysis or other means. The game developers could sell data directly to end consumers or license it to a data feed company as the NFL, MLB, and NBA do.

ESPORTS VENUES eSports facilities are already being created by universities, game developers, and professional eSports teams. Traditional sports bars like Dave & Buster's and movie theaters like Cinemark have eSports nights. There will likely be much growth in independent, local eSports venues, which will be a cross between an arcade and sports bar and cater to the 16–25-year-old market. Over time, these venues will consolidate into national chains like traditional sports bars.

FAN EXPERIENCE ENHANCEMENT This segment will likely evolve along similar lines as traditional pro sports, including improved stadium experiences, companion mobile analytics, and virtual and augmented reality. The determinants of adoption depend on the league, venue, and game developers.

MARKETING METRICS This area is already starting to flourish as more people follow eSports. Digital media companies specialize in this space to track viewing and optimize marketing techniques.

MOBILE GAMES While the entry costs are dramatically increasing, the sheer growth and volume will create many opportunities as hand and body sensor costs decline. Mobile games will become the dominant medium with huge bandwidth developing through 5G emerging networks and lower-cost virtual and augmented reality equipment.

4

Youth Sports

Overview

Youth sports of today are so different from the games of my childhood. The days of only baseball, football, and basketball are gone. Youth sports have moved from a family's side activity to, in many cases, a family's main priority. Money and culture have changed sports. Youth sports were once the domain of sleepy recreation centers, YMCAs, and schools. Now, multimillion-dollar nonprofit and for-profit enterprises have raised the competition level dramatically while shoe and apparel companies add jet fuel to grow the fire. Then COVID-19 led to a dramatic reset of the segment. Unsurprisingly, 2020 participation rates fell dramatically. But before we address the reset, let's explore the underlying conditions. We will quote 2019 figures as 2020 figures are distorted.

According to *The Atlantic*, youth sports spending is nearly $17 billion, bigger than professional baseball and comparable to the NFL. According to the Sports & Fitness Industry Association (SFIA), youth aged six to twelve who play a sport on a regular basis fell from 49 percent in 2012 to 37 percent in 2020. However, the story is more troubling when using an income filter. According to SFIA, 43 percent of children in that age bracket in families earning greater than $100,000 played a sport while just 24 percent of children from families earning less than $25,000 did. In 2012, 34 percent of children of low-resource families played a sport. In short, children of wealthier families continue to play sports while children from low-resource families play fewer sports. The trend line is similar for children aged thirteen to eighteen.

According to SFIA, only six youth sports—cycling, basketball, baseball, soccer, football, and tennis—have more than one million participants who are six to twelve years old (see figure 4.1). Each sport's growth has its own story.

Cycling is the largest participatory sport with 4.8 million children. However, the trend has dramatically declined since 2008. The percentage of participants six to twelve years old has fallen from 28 percent in 2008 to 17 percent in 2019. However, the pandemic has created a boom in cycling, given the sport was one of the few activities in which families and children could still participate.

Some organizations are taking a different approach. While cycling has huge youth participation rates, there are limited cycling competitions in middle and high school. The National Interscholastic Cycling Association (NICA) fosters the development of mountain bike racing teams in middle and high schools. In the last decade, the nonprofit has developed over twenty state chapters with over eighteen thousand student-athletes. However, the NICA is an example of a high-growth enterprise thriving in youth sports despite declining trends in the sport.

Youth football is experiencing a dramatic change. In 2019, high school football participation had decreased for ten out of the last eleven years to approximately one million. From 2008 to 2020, tackle football participation among youth six to twelve declined to 780,000. Concerns over head injuries are cited as the most common reason. But there is good news. During 2019, the number of kids of that age playing flag football grew by 6.8 percent to 940,000. That group represents more than those who currently play tackle football, according to a study by SFIA. The Aspen Institute has led the call for kids to start tackle football after the age of fourteen. In 2017, the NFL pledged to award annual grants to four hundred Boys & Girls Clubs for flag football programs with the goal of reaching one hundred thousand players aged six to eighteen. The league-owned NFL Network now broadcasts national flag football tournaments.

Percentage of children ages 6-12 who participated on a regular basis in 2021
(number of days varies by sport)

Sport		2008	2019	2020	2021	2020-2021 Change	# Kids in 2021
	Baseball	16.5%	14.4%	12.2%	12.6%	3.0%	3,670,506
	Basketball	16.6%	14.0%	14.8%	14.5%	-2.3%	4,208,369
	Bicycling	27.7%	17.0%	18.2%	18.0%	-0.9%	5,243,326
	Cheerleading	2.4%	2.9%	2.3%	2.2%	-2.6%	649,347
	Flag Football	4.5%	3.5%	3.4%	3.4%	1.5%	1,000,296
	Tackle Football	3.7%	2.9%	2.8%	2.3%	-17.9%	677,872
	Golf	5.0%	4.6%	5.3%	5.2%	-1.9%	1,500,000
	Gymnastics	2.3%	3.6%	2.9%	3.0%	4.2%	881,905
	Ice Hockey	0.5%	1.2%	1.0%	0.9%	-10.5%	272,662
	Lacrosse	0.4%	1.0%	0.9%	0.7%	-23.7%	200,509
	Soccer (Outdoor)	10.4%	7.7%	6.2%	7.4%	19.5%	2,160,186
	Softball (Fast-Pitch)	1.0%	1.4%	1.2%	1.2%	-0.1%	348,575
	Swimming (Team)	N/A	1.3%	1.0%	1.1%	11.9%	334,394
	Tennis	4.3%	4.3%	5.9%	5.8%	-2.9%	1,681,717
	Track and Field	1.0%	1.1%	1.2%	1.1%	-7.3%	322,862
	Volleyball (Court)	2.9%	2.9%	2.5%	2.6%	4.8%	751,197

Figure 4.1.
Core participation in select sports.

Source: Project Play, The Aspen Institute, https://www.aspenprojectplay.org/youth-sports
/facts/participation-rates.
Data from the Sports & Fitness Industry Association.

After declining participation, baseball and softball have experienced a resurgence. Baseball participation has grown 21 percent since 2014. According to SFIA, the number of players from age six to college level reached 15.9 million in 2018. The *Wall Street Journal* cites that casual players who play up to twelve times a year represent the largest growth, while the frequent-player growth rate was only 5 percent. The uptick in the sport is attributed to joint initiatives by the MLB, USA Softball, and USA Baseball. The MLB's "Play Ball" program's goal is simple: it aims to get kids swinging bats and throwing balls. It reminds people that they do not need a formal team and referees to enjoy themselves. A small casual game can be fun and help children learn the basics. The joint initiative has also launched a nationwide program to teach schoolchildren in kindergarten to the fourth grade.

Though NBA viewership is flat, youth basketball participation (ages six to seventeen) grew 4 percent to 7.7 million players in 2020. The NBA has codeveloped a grassroots program for young players and local coaches. The website provides a curriculum of how-to videos with NBA stars to provide some sizzle. Sponsored events balance the online presence of the program.

While professional soccer viewership is growing, youth participation is surprisingly declining. According to SFIA, from 2008 to 2019, the percentage of kids six to twelve playing soccer dropped by 35 percent to 1.7 million players. Unsurprisingly, soccer draws from predominantly wealthy families, with heavy representation in the suburbs. Households making more than $100,000 in annual income provide 35 percent of players, while only 11 percent come from households earning $25,000 or less. Other explanations include burnout associated with annual tryouts, "bulldozer" parenting, and more sports options.

After being known as one of the fastest-growing sports, ultimate frisbee participation has slowed considerably. USA Ultimate member growth slowed to 1 percent in 2018 after enjoying double-digit growth in previous years. The sport faces challenges in growing out of the mostly male, 18–24-year-old core segment.

Several nontraditional sports—ice hockey and lacrosse—are experiencing remarkable growth though the base is very small. According to USA Hockey, participation numbers in 2019 reached 567,908 compared to 195,125 players in 1990, an increase of 190 percent. Female hockey players reached 80,000 nationally. Gymnastics and track and field are enjoying a modest revival.

Obesity is a disturbing trend in youth sports and it's decreasing the pool of youth athletes. According to the Henry J. Kaiser Family Foundation, 31 percent of youth ten to seventeen years old are either overweight (eighty-fifth to ninety-fifth percentile body mass index) or obese (higher than the ninety-fifth percentile). This figure is consistent with the U.S. Army's report that 31 percent of potential soldiers are rejected due to obesity. These trends predate adult patterns. According to the CDC, 32 percent of adults are overweight (their BMI is 25–30 percent), and 40 percent of adults are obese (their BMI is greater than 30 percent). Income and location are driving factors. Growing obesity is often attributed to the wide availability of high-calorie foods and drinks, gaming, and screens.

This trend will likely have a huge impact on youth sports going forward. The fact is that 31 percent of youth and 72 percent of adults are either overweight or obese. While this trend could get somewhat worse, I expect a correction as health care costs are growing beyond our means. Obesity is a key driver of the health care crisis in the United States. Economics will drive the change. Government intervention—food and drink taxes and regulation—will likely occur to offset the single-digit annual cost increases. These actions may cause great economic opportunities for enterprises working on youth sports, as illustrated in figure 4.2.

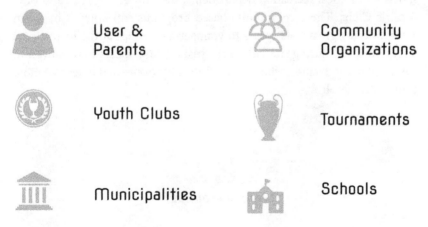

Figure 4.2.
Youth ecosystem.

Schools

Contrary to popular opinion, there has not been a significant decline in PE class attendance. According to the National Physical Activity Plan Alliance, 50 percent of high school students attended PE classes during 1991–2015. That being said, half of the students taking PE class seems like a woeful number. School used to be the ultimate domain of youth sports. These varsity sports have been under siege as school district funding declines along with the number of high school varsity athletes. Based on an annual report of the National Federation of State High School Associations, high school sports participation declined during the 2018–2019 season for the first time in thirty years. Football participation led to the decline.

Community Organizations

For many years during the twentieth century, the sole domain of youth sports was at local recreation departments, the YMCA, the JCC, and Boys & Girls Clubs. These community-based programs still flourish in urban areas, offering grassroots sports to younger age groups at the recreational level. However, during the last thirty years, youth sports have moved to pay-to-play youth clubs, who then shift the kids twelve and older to a more competitive level.

Municipalities

Historically, municipalities have paid the lion's share for youth sports by offering sports in school and providing low-cost parks and recreation leagues on municipal fields and courts. Here to stay, however, the pay-to-play youth model provides the greatest advantages to wealthy families. Clubs often offer scholarships for the highest-performing athletes, while some clubs offer waivers for those who cannot afford the fees.

There is a great need to increase youth physical activity, particularly among those families who cannot afford the pay-to-play models. Local municipalities will likely be greatly constrained in providing more financial resources. Federal support seems complicated on many levels.

One novel approach has been proposed by Tom Cove, CEO of SFIA. He suggests that tax revenue from sports betting should go toward youth sports and physical fitness.

Youth Clubs

Pay-to-play clubs have become more prominent. Travel teams in baseball, basketball, soccer, rugby, and lacrosse are creating pathways to college and pro sports. For example, U.S. Soccer's Development Academy has become the recruiting mainstay for NCAA Division 1 and Division 3 college soccer programs; it even prohibits its athletes from playing on any high school sports teams. The model of a separate school and sports academy is common in Europe and South America. The move to a separate sports academy will likely create more favorable opportunities for youth sports enterprises.

While most of the clubs are nonprofits, they have the DNA of private enterprise. The clubs have professionalized many of the key work processes. Software has greatly simplified registration, tryouts, scheduling, team communications, and tournament management. Liability insurance is offered by national sports associations that compete for club members. New clubs are often required to join oligarchical state sports associations to compete against existing association member teams.

Management and staff are often recruited from private enterprises. They bring best corporate practices. Club cultures are more intentionally curated. Front line staff and coaches are more focused on customer service. Stakeholder relationships—field owners, apparel and shoe companies, college coaches, and orthopedic clinics—are more effectively managed. Coaches obtain certificates from their respective national sports associations. Elite coaches move toward full-time employment with a large pool of part-time coaches. Successful clubs have their own physical trainers and strength and agility coaches. Clubs develop off-season and additional in-season training sessions to create a year-round offering to the consumer.

As each sport evolves, there is pyramidal segmentation. Recreation for the youngest kids is the base of the pyramid. The next level splits between school and club. Within the club level, there are various levels, with the tip of the pyramid being national team players.

With the exception of football, the path to college sports is increasingly through club teams. National associations and apparel companies create annual academy showcases and tournaments to feature high-level talent. College coaches find annual showcases easier than attending a multitude of high school events.

Tournaments

Tournaments have become the main fixture in youth sports and the communities around them. Clubs can generate an additional 10–20 percent in fees annually. Towns and municipalities have become very supportive of multiday tournaments as a means of economic development. While nationally aggregated data is hard to find, municipalities often report annual results. According to the website Visit South Bend Mishawaka, the Compton Family Ice Arena—home arena to the University of Notre Dame men's hockey team—hosted or cohosted twenty-six youth hockey events during the 2018–19 academic year. They report that these events contributed $12.5 million to the local economy. For small towns such as Saginaw, Michigan, regional soccer tournaments bring in up to $15 million. According to ABC 12, a six-day soccer event in June brings in an estimated fifteen thousand people, which has a dramatic effect on local hotels, restaurants, and entertainment venues.

However, not all projects work out smoothly. Grand Park in Westfield, Indiana, welcomes nearly 1.5 million visitors annually. The outdoor sports campus features thirty-one multipurpose fields (for soccer, football, and lacrosse) and twenty-six baseball and softball diamonds. According to the research firm Applied Economics, the park generated $150 million in economic activity in 2015. The Indianapolis suburb paid $57 million to build the outdoor fields and eventually purchase the land. While Grand Park is generating a great deal of economic activity, much of the activity is in neighboring towns. The park itself operates at a modest loss. Time will tell if the project is successful as other towns—nearby Fishers and Portage—in the state open venues.

Sports camp information on the national level is difficult to find. However, the economic impact for coaches and staff is considerable as they need income during the off-season.

Constraints

SUBJECT MATTER EXPERTISE The coaches of the sport must be experts. It is not enough to be a former college or pro player, though that experience helps.

LOCAL KNOWLEDGE The business owners must understand the local ecosystem and also have relationships with other clubs, recreation departments, field owners, state organizations, and national associations.

FIELD ACCESS The owners must have a clear idea of how to obtain field and court space and which clubs have priority.

COACHES They need to have access to and relationships with local coaches.

CERTIFICATIONS Organizations and coaches require both state and national accreditation.

INCREASED PROFESSIONALIZATION Best business practices and benchmarks will need to be applied to youth organizations.

BUILD COMMUNITY Organizations create their own "tribe" so that their customers are highly loyal.

GROW NEW SPORTS Niche sports without existing infrastructure and competitors will require development.

ANCILLARY SERVICES The organization must offer speed, strength, and agility training along with sports psychology and orthopedic and rehabilitation services.

Opportunities

COVID-19 will be the biggest inflection point in youth sports for the foreseeable future. According to the Aspen Institute, 20–40 percent of youth clubs will go out of business due to the virus. Organizations operating on the margin will fail. Subscale clubs or large clubs with poor finances will be found out. Most likely, only the largest clubs with buffers and the scrappiest clubs will survive. Emerging trends—like online and offline offerings and supplemental training—will accelerate. Supplemental trainers—private coaches, especially those with a digital presence—have likely seen a boom in business or a great willingness for families to spend on their services. New winners will emerge. . . .

The recession will drive down disposable family income leading to a slower bounceback. Families will likely opt for more local solutions as the overhang from a lower income and fear of traveling. Now may be the best time in the last thirty years to get into youth sports since it may be difficult in the foreseeable future.

NEW CLUB CREATION This is an obvious choice if you are a coach or club director with deep local contacts. Opportunities always present themselves if existing clubs are not providing adequate customer service or are poorly executing. Starting clubs is generally hard as it requires either taking away customers from existing clubs or building awareness of new sports. Most are nonprofits in order to take advantage of lower-cost field rentals and save on taxes. I am generally skeptical of new clubs being created in the traditional sports—basketball, tackle football, soccer, hockey, and baseball. It is really difficult to disrupt the incumbent clubs, particularly as state associations generally protect existing clubs. You will need a special advantage to pry away other clubs' customers and coaches. Equally important, you will need to get access to fields as most existing clubs will likely have their own or a long-term relationship with their municipalities. However, COVID-19 will cull existing clubs and create opportunities in different regions.

There are opportunities for new clubs for nontraditional sports—lacrosse, ultimate frisbee, and rugby—though these enterprises will face unique challenges. Building awareness for the sport will require a longer runway. Obtaining field access from municipalities will be an uphill battle. State and national association certification will likely be easier.

Many new clubs are formed in part because founders have children who want to play the sport. This passion helps justify the likely below-market returns that they will receive for their efforts and investment. If the enterprise scales, then the return may be worth all the work. For new clubs, the local conditions will drive success, plain and simple. The challenge is to make the right decision on how many dots can be connected cost effectively. Though often not scalable outside their local markets, sports clubs can be a consistent cash flow generator as a nonprofit or for-profit organization.

SUPPLEMENTAL SERVICES Both sports clubs or third parties can offer supplemental holiday or off-season camps, private training, and speed and agility training. Rehab or orthopedic services can be provided by third parties. For emerging sports, tournaments can be offered on a broader scale to include entertainment and food. Enterprising food trucks can benefit from the large crowds at tournaments or even regular evening practices. COVID-19 likely had an accelerating impact on these services as families are more open to new approaches to sport.

YOUTH LEAGUE AND MANAGEMENT SOFTWARE Some opportunities exist for this category. We are in version 3.0, where the basic offering was made during version 1.0, and competitors presented refined offerings in version 2.0. The remaining opportunities exist for emerging sports management, which has unique needs. I do think that there is a large unmet gap for online sports training, which has libraries of training plans and private coaching services in nearly all sports. We have some time until this type of training mainstreams, but there is no reason why guided personalized online training should not grow dramatically.

Personal Startup

I didn't like the idea, but I promised that I would look at the business plan. A well-intentioned soccer dad asked me to look over a plan for a soccer training facility with four fields. After a fairly quick look, I knew that the math did not make sense. Four artificial turf fields with lights could cost at least $4 million. Field rentals are about $120 a game. It would take many years to pay off the fields, likely beyond the usable lifetime of the turf.

During our boys' practice, I explained that financing of these projects was best left to municipalities who could take a longer view. Private money would not. When we were wrapping up, I asked about a little box in the rendering that said school. He said that he liked the idea of having a school where kids could train in the morning, attend classes, and train in the afternoon and evening. The goal would be to find kids crazy about soccer who had fun training twice as much as their peers. Bam! A lightning bolt of an idea struck me. All of a sudden I was interested. Here's why.

My first startup was an early childhood education training center. I had just stepped down from the board of a local public school nonprofit. While the district was one of the top ranked in the state and country, I became disillusioned at the slow pace that education best practices were being implemented.

The downside of a school is the cost of building the campus. While beautiful buildings in tranquil settings are lovely, caring teachers and an adaptive curriculum drive academic success. I had a clear idea of teacher compensation from my board work. I looked into several online curriculums. I knew that students could learn some subjects better online since the technology never tires of explaining the material while progress only happens once topics are mastered. I felt that a hybrid curriculum—both small in-person classes and online—was the best approach based on the education research available.

The next challenge was finding reputable coaches parents would trust. The soccer dad had already been speaking with a high-level Division 1 soccer coach in the area who had a son our son's age. He was a U.S. National Team player and one of the first Americans to play in the English First Division, which later became the Premier League.

The final element was finding a place to host the school and training fields. By luck, there was an outstanding practice facility not far away. The luxury boxes were flex spaces that could host a classroom. The town and state were incredibly supportive of the project to bring a soccer-focused school—like an IMG sports academy—to central North Carolina. The local pro team signed up to support the effort.

Once those stars aligned, the real work began. We had to find fifteen students whose families were willing to take a chance on their children's education and pay tuition. We reached out to the three local soccer clubs. They were supportive but did not push the project too aggressively with their customers. We attended soccer tryouts with limited success. Parents were much more focused on which teams their children made. After a great deal of talking to families one-on-one, we were able to sign up enough students for the first year. We hired two teachers, one of whom was a mom of one of the students.

Over time, we learned that families first signed up for the soccer but stayed because of the small classroom size. Though we expanded to middle and high school, our student body only grew to about twenty students. One of the local clubs partnered with the public school district to create a competitor high school program.

After four years, we were offered the opportunity to move to a new facility and add hockey players to the program. As a result, our school size doubled. The culture and energy improved even more. Over time, the school created locations in other large U.S. cities and one in Spain. After six years, I exited the business as another well-intentioned parent wanted to take a larger role. I also realize that I am a creator, not a maintainer. After six years it felt right to step aside for a team with fresh ideas.

The school was a fabulous startup in that we were able to create an outstanding learning and training environment for our kids and other families who believed in the vision. We certainly validated the demand for an alternative learning environment; COVID-19 opened parents' eyes to more than one way of educating students in a traditional classroom and schedule. I would hardly call remote learning during the pandemic successful; schools were really offering emergency remote learning. But the perception had changed. We are seeing public school systems further exploring hybrid and remote learning in the same way we did several years ago.

The school was hard to scale because of the perception that school needs to be taught traditionally. Some key stakeholders, namely youth clubs, were very helpful while others were not. Soccer training can get very territorial. After six years, we still could not get full buy-in from every-one. Social media marketing over the years did not move the needle for us. Word of mouth worked well but we have such a small base. Small scale education will never make much money; parents rightfully demanded a great deal of attention given the tuition they were paying.

Given the changed perception and fresh leadership, the Accelerator School has great promise. From a market perspective, we might have been too early to scale from hobby to business. However, from an impact per-spective, especially on our kids, we may have started too late. I like their chances.

Interview

Tom Farrey—Sports & Society Program at the Aspen Institute
San Clemente, California

Tom is amazing at telling stories. He should be, since he has been a journalist since high school in South Florida. He is a thought leader in youth sports in America, and his canvas is broad. Tom has an edge that only comes from being fundamentally relentless. This quality likely served him well as an investigative journalist for ESPN. Entrepreneurs have the same attribute. He looks at youth sports from many lenses: someone who played them as a child, a journalist who has spoken to so many athletes and coaches, and a parent of three children. Tom is ringing the alarm on the growing gaps in our youth sport communities. He sees these gaps as opportunities to fix some big societal problems in education and health.

CHRIS: Tom, tell me about yourself.

TOM: I'm a kid of the 1970s and South Florida, where I grew up ten blocks from the beach. I played a lot of sports when I was younger but prob-ably slipped on a uniform at age eight. Most of my sports activity was unstructured free play. I went to the beach every weekend with my parents. I would jump over the waves pretending that I was Mer-cury Morris, the great running back of the Miami Dolphins. As I got older, I would sneak onto a local golf course after school, hoping that the course rangers didn't chase me off the course. My friends and I would play football, baseball, and basketball. While never great,

I developed a love of sport and appreciation for its ability to develop human beings.

As I got older, this appreciation grounded me in exploring larger themes in our society—race, gender, sex, politics, violence, and globalization—through the lens of sports. Fortunately, I got a part-time job at the *Miami Herald* during high school. I really enjoyed professional storytelling, which led to an internship at the *Los Angeles Times* and then an early job at the *Seattle Times* covering the NBA and the NFL.

I quickly transitioned into investigative reporting. I left in 1986 to be part of the group that built what would become espn.com. I got excited about helping create a new medium. During my twenty-one years at ESPN and *Outside the Lines*, I was a senior writer for the magazine. I traveled all over the world and asked lots of interesting people questions that I would ordinarily never get a chance to ask them. It was an amazing job as a journalist. I would write about what I learned from these interesting people, and my paycheck showed up in the mail.

In 2008, I wrote this book called *Game on: The All-American Race to Make Champions of Our Children*. The book was a journalistic survey of the landscape of youth sports in America. The experience got me thinking about solutions, namely how to build a better sports system in this country. I wanted to explore how to get more kids off the couch into sports without running them into the ground. The goal was to help create effective citizens and healthy communities through sport. Over time, that interest led me to transition from ESPN to the Aspen Institute, where I created the sports and society program. Our signature initiative, Project Play, is focused on building healthy communities through sports. I stay active in mountain biking, tennis, beach volleyball, and surfing with my friends and sons.

CHRIS: So how has your perception of youth sports changed watching your children play sports?

TOM: Well, I have two sons. My eldest son, Cole, was both a basketball and soccer player, later playing soccer at Division 3 Babson College, an entrepreneurship-focused school outside of Boston. My youngest son, Kellen, is also a soccer player and dabbles in tennis.

While I did a full autopsy of our youth sports system, I applied my learning to find the best practical ways that I could support my children in navigating the sports landscape. These ideas include multisport play, love of the game, physical literacy, and the value of quality coaching.

CHRIS: What are some top-of-mind secular trends that you see in youth sports?

TOM: The biggest trend is the separation between haves and have-nots over the past thirty years. Think about a privatized recreation environment where private club teams have the best training options and get scouted. Families who don't have the money can't make it work. We see lots of lower-income kids not playing sports these days, or at least not having a sustained sporting experience. The factors include kids having to take care of family or work responsibilities, school demands, or transportation struggles.

On the opposite end, the privatized recreation environment leads kids to be fed sports with a fire hose. There is an epidemic of overuse injuries, excessive concussions to some degree, high burnout rates, and performance anxiety. The kids know that their parents are looking for a return on investment for all this money, time, and energy. Our system was dysfunctional at best and broken at worst. COVID-19 has only exposed those fundamental flaws and deficiencies.

CHRIS: The emergence of the "youth sports industrial complex" has a tremendous impact on the haves and the have-nots. That trend is pervasive, not only in sports but also in education, and is probably in every element of the economy. One hopes in the United States is that education and youth sports still have some sort of equal opportunity. How can we fix the youth sports' inequities if those prevailing themes are in the overall economy and culture?

TOM: First, we need to fix this manic impulse to sort the weak from the strong before kids hit puberty and grow into their bodies, minds, and interests. We live in a competitive society. We live in a capitalistic society. We want people to reap the rewards of hard work. It's counterproductive and unfair to have travel teams before the age of twelve. You don't even know who is going to be a good athlete at that point. All that is known is that the families can afford travel teams. That experience ends up dominating the youth sports environment in this country. These youth end up getting looks from college scouts after being aggregated in tournaments.

We as a community just need to commit to giving every kid at least until age twelve an opportunity to develop physical literacy, love of the game, and multisport experience. The focus should be on the fun with developmentally appropriate play under the supervision of coaches who know what they're doing. The stakes are high. The research shows that less active kids are more likely to be obese and more likely to suffer chronic diseases. Less active kids are less likely to stay in school, go to college, and make good money. Active kids are likely to be active parents, which means that they are likely to be more active role models for their kids. We have to commit to triggering the virtuous cycle that occurs if kids stay active.

CHRIS: The sports venue for kids before age twelve has historically been schools. But the value of physical education has been diminished as higher academic standards are trying to be achieved. Where do you see the opportunity?

TOM: We are in the post-COVID moment with new opportunities. We've got to recenter the sport experience on forms of play that are local, affordable, and high quality. The societal payoff will be huge from a public policy and investment point of view. The main leverage is at the parks and recreation departments that control the community sports spaces. They can prioritize programs that are affordable and high quality. It is hard to achieve both of those goals. However, grantmakers can align their criteria to support local parks and recreation departments, YMCAs, and Boys & Girls Clubs. These need to be key institutions. As a community, we should commit to those local opportunities and find multiple investing partners such as governors, foundations, corporations, and the federal government. It is a stimulus investment that has long-term returns in economic and education dollars.

Schools will continue to play a major role by providing high-quality physical education. The priorities have to evolve from supporting just the best athletes in the school to democratizing sport for all students. While you can still aspire to have competitive varsity teams, the priority should be on broader intramural events for all students. The broader adoption of being physically active promotes good academics and improved cognitive function, which leads to greater educational outcomes.

The role of PE teachers will dramatically evolve into chief sports officers of their community. They will have relationships with the clubs and leagues in the community. These PE teachers can make evaluations and provide parents with a menu of options based on the physical and psychosocial needs of the students. I think there's a lot of room for innovation. We just launched a competition where we will hand out $160,000 to schools that are the most exemplary models. We need to rethink the models.

CHRIS: Given that there are a fixed number of hours in a school day, what do you cut to allow for more physical activity? Where are the threads of optimism?

TOM: It's going to take real shifts in the model; we can't tweak the system hoping that we will achieve systemic results. We need to look at extending the school day. Schools don't have to be the providers of everything as they don't have the facilities, space, or staff capacity. Local community organizations are open to those kinds of partnerships. The first step is to connect the silos and see what's possible. The second step is to have a community conversation about if sports are important and whether we should make them co-curricular. It just takes being bold and a willingness to shift the model. It's a huge challenge focusing on thousands of kids' well-being versus a few hundred varsity athletes. Parents are open to models that are going to deliver greater outcomes for a wider swath of the student population. We will need to have really big conversations.

CHRIS: I think most people will agree that more youth playing sports is good. How specifically do parks and recreation departments play a role in this tremendous change?

TOM: It comes down to the power of the permit. These departments control the facilities or the hardware. Some also control the coaching or software. Goals and metrics can be established for each facility. These metrics could include coaching quality, affordability, safety protocols, number of free/reduced lunch participants, and zip code. The permit can be the key lever in youth sports to incentivize youth clubs to be broader based.

CHRIS: So I'm going to push back a bit. In my local area, the YMCA, the JCC, and Boys & Girls Clubs do a pretty good job of providing low-cost sporting opportunities for children under twelve years old. Is that the experience nationally, or is the need not being met?

TOM: In past years, YMCAs served kids until sixth grade or so. Now, they lose students by second grade. Oftentimes, better-off families just flee to the privatized clubs. Your local one might be good because you live in a very educated and relatively wealthy area. The quality of YMCAs and Boys & Girls Clubs is all over the map.

YMCAs serve kids at scale from all backgrounds. As the private club environment develops, it takes resources away from these community organizations that are under pressure to break even. There is tremendous pressure to cater to families who have cash. Every organization says that they offer scholarships to those deserving kids in need. But do scholarships work? Nobody really knows. There is little research on the topic. The program skims the cream off the top—the best athletes—while doing little for the much larger base who will become parents and citizens. I'm not convinced that it's a way to drive sports participation in scale.

CHRIS: Youth participation in traditional sports is in decline. There's been some bounceback in baseball. Some would say it's because MLB has invested a lot in grassroots efforts. The NBA is doing a similar program. Do you think it's sustainable? Or are we going to continue to see steady declines in traditional sports?

TOM: Honestly, I don't think anything is inevitable. It will come down to leadership and coherent strategies and aligning programming more with the interests of kids. If that's done frequently within team sports, then traditional team sports will be fine. Kids want to be around their friends because they want to have a group experience, especially when they're younger. If the kids are segmented at a young age, and only the best get playing time, then the experience is not good for the rest. At younger ages, we can redesign team sports to be more child-development-centric.

Let's agree on the goals and the metrics. I could go on and on about the number of efforts out there to create a better experience. The NBA has really done terrific things in recent years. But if things don't change fundamentally, then I can see newer individual sports with more free play replacing team sports.

CHRIS: I completely agree with the need to be athlete-centric. Sports need to be open to evolving to the current reality and needs. Baseball was developed in an age where agriculture was predominant and the land was cheap. Why can't sports evolve so they are easier to play? Bigger goals and fewer players on smaller fields in soccer. Bigger holes and shorter courses in golf. Faster baseball games with more runs. We can keep the purist version in some areas, but we have to recognize the constraints of the twenty-first century. Facilities are expensive. I think sports need to evolve, so we serve a broader population. I also see a need to offer new sports to reflect the diversification of youth interests. What are you seeing?

TOM: COVID-19 generated a boom in individual sports: cycling, surfing, tennis, and the PGA. The PGA has done good work on teen golf in that it's not just one kid competing against everyone else, but you're on a team. Tennis organizations also recognize the value; it's a great opportunity for a reset. It's going to be a real challenge to get dads to change their mindset about what a sport is or should be.

CHRIS: What trends do you see accelerating or terminating due to COVID-19?

TOM: Schools have less money to provide sports as money goes to sanitation. We have to make sports a priority in youth education. These tradeoffs may lead to dropping certain sports or modifying them, or shortening seasons. I don't know exactly how it'll come out. There will be some schools that react in a really innovative, next-generation way. Many others are going to just double down on the old way and hope to ride it out.

CHRIS: I want to circle back on the notion of having both a democratized sports environment and an elite environment. How can we balance this democratization for kids before twelve years old and elite sports?

TOM: We need to commit ourselves to offer quality multisport experiences accessible to all kids under age twelve. Kids want to play with other kids. Everyone benefits. We want to have a conversation with parents that sports participation develops health, social and emotional skills, resilience, character, and all the good stuff that we think sports produce. We can discuss college scholarships or pro sports opportunities later.

5

Fitness

Overview

This segment has been a hotbed for entrepreneurial activity during the last thirty years. In the 1970 and 1980s, the fitness category meant gyms, exercise videos, and weights. At times, the segment seemed mature. But it has been reinvented with new entrants finding traction by offering differentiated experiences and services. Technology and community building have been the two main driving forces. According to the International Health, Racquet & Sportsclub Association, there are about forty thousand clubs with sixty-two million members in the United States. Net membership growth and member retention were 2.4 percent and 71.4 percent, respectively, while visits surpassed five billion. Fitness club revenue already exceeds $30 billion nationally. Nonprofits, such as the YMCA and JCC, represent about five thousand of the forty thousand clubs.

Keep in mind that only one-third of the U.S. total population is active in health fitness. Currently, two-thirds of U.S. adults are either overweight or obese. Something has to change.

COVID-19 reset the landscape in fitness with the role of the termina-tor and accelerator. Middle-market players will not survive the protracted economic downturn. Large, well-capitalized chains will survive the Great Pause and thrive during the recovery with less competition. Other win-ners will include specialized studio offerings with an adaptive mindset, low overheads, remote offerings, or strong community engagement. The churn will create a great number of opportunities for those with the experience, capital, and network.

Brief History

The notion of the modern gym is likely grounded in the growth of Gold's Gym in the 1970s. Located in Venice Beach, California, the modest, under-capitalized gym was the setting for the movie *Pumping Iron* (1977). The film highlighted the 1975 Mr. Universe and Mr. Olympia bodybuilding competitions with highly charismatic stars such as Arnold Schwarzeneg-ger and Lou Ferrigno. The movie inspired a generation of amateur weight-lifters while Gold's Gym expanded to over five hundred locations around the world. Schwarzenegger's movie *Conan the Barbarian* likely inspired a generation of weight lifters. Numerous independent gyms were eventually consolidated into large national chains like LA Fitness, Life Time Fitness, and Crunch Fitness.

During the 1970s, Jazzercise offered a dance-meets-exercise regimen for women. Though founded in Evanston, Illinois, the concept flourished in Carlsbad, California. The company has over 8,300 franchises in thirty-two countries with numerous video offerings. The curriculum was emu-lated in dance classes in other gyms, YMCAs, and JCCs.

In 1995, Golftec launched studios where sensors are attached to clients to track body part angles and speeds to improve golf swings. Personal fit-ness tracking devices emerged around 2000. Suunto and Garmin were the first movers focused on the running, triathlete, and outdoor segment dur-ing the early 2000s. Fitbit and Apple Watch were driven to provide fitness devices to the mainstream through heart rate monitoring, steps walked, and sleep quality.

This hardware innovation helped fuel a mobile app revolution that includes TrainingPeaks, Strava, and MapMyRide. The mobile apps provide different elements: goal setting, route suggestions, customizable training plans, and community competitions. During the last five years, there has been an explosion of personal fitness apps for home-based weightlifting, yoga, and general fitness. These include MyFitnessPal, Workout for Women, 30 Day Fitness, and 7 Minute Workout. In addition, more detailed web applications specializing in sports niches—such as speed training (Lee Taft) or soccer footwork (Renegade Soccer)—are offering lifetime subscriptions for $200–$700.

Key Players

The key players in fitness are illustrated in figure 5.1.

 Big Box Fitness

 Home-based Fitness

 Equipment Makers

 Devices

 Community-based Fitness

Figure 5.1.
Fitness ecosystem.

Big Box Fitness

These megachains are the latest generation to offer everything to the widest possible target audience with an affordable, relatively easy-to-cancel contract.

PLANET FITNESS

Planet Fitness differentiates itself by offering a "judgment free zone" and focuses on new or occasional fitness members at an attractive monthly fee. Founded in 1993, the organization has grown to over 1,800 locations and was bought out by TSG Consumer Partners private equity firm in 2013.

LA FITNESS

Founded in 1983, LA Fitness fueled much of its growth by purchasing underperforming gyms in key markets. While opening new clubs has grown the business, the purchase of 171 clubs from Bally Total Fitness drove its expansion.

24 HOUR FITNESS

Founded in 1983, 24 Hour Fitness operates over 420 locations with 24/7 access.

Equipment Makers/Retailers

Schwinn was one of the first companies to offer aerobic equipment. Exercise bikes, treadmills, and elliptical machines have gone through many evolutions with a multitude of brands. Some lasted while many didn't make it.

NORDIC TRACK

Since 1975, NordicTrack has offered Nordic ski machines, treadmills, and elliptical machines direct to the consumer. After a disastrous foray into retail, the company was purchased when it went bankrupt in 1998. Since then, the company has focused on value-oriented treadmills.

PRECOR

Founded as a rowing machine company in 1980, Precor is a market leader in treadmills and elliptical machines. The company was an early adopter in adding computer chips and video to machines.

Community-based Fitness

CROSSFIT

CrossFit was founded in 2000, and the program is a combination of exercise philosophy and sports competition. The training is a combination of high-intensity intervals, gymnastics, plyometric training, and strongman exercises. With twelve thousand affiliated gyms, CrossFit has a Workout of the Day (WOD) and uses a virtual community model. The gyms offer hourly workout programs. The regimen has been adopted by military and law enforcement, and men and women are represented equally in membership.

SOULCYCLE

Founded in 2006, Soul Cycle is an indoor cycling studio company with eighty-nine locations in the United States and the UK. Charging $30+ for a forty-five-minute class, the company has taken the user experience to the next level. The founding team included the right expertise of a spin instructor, a real estate agent with capital, and a talent manager. With stylish, candlelit studios, charismatic instructors lead high-intensity spin classes with a combination of personalization, storytelling, therapy, and community building. The instructors, who go through a rigorous interview process and two-month training, including hospitality, achieve virtual cultlike status by their savvy use of social media. In 2011, the company was purchased by Equinox Gym for a potential IPO. Soul Cycle has been a thought leader creating a premium user experience, charismatic instructors, and a strong community.

ORANGETHEORY FITNESS

Orangetheory offers group training classes that combine high-intensity interval training and strength training. Founded in 2010, the franchisor has over a thousand locations worldwide. The intense group environment is a key differentiator.

Home-based Fitness

PELOTON

Peloton has taken the high-end spin class to the next level through technology, and it takes place in the convenience of your home. The problem that the company wanted to solve was how people could take great classes without traveling to the studio. Founded in 2011, the company primarily sells delivered spin bikes for about $2,250 and a $39 monthly subscription. The screen on the bike allows users to watch the live or recorded training sessions, track their heart rate and participate in the community. Dubbed the "Netflix of Fitness" by *Forbes* magazine, Peloton offers more than fifteen live classes with multicamera studio production in cycling, running, yoga, strength, and cardio. The instructors have great energy, and the music is dialed in. The results are amazing: one million users, four hundred thousand bikes purchased, and a $4 billion valuation as it expands aggressively into other sports products, such as treadmills. Other companies—such as the connected rowing machine startups Hydrow and CityRow—have emulated the cycling business model for rowing. Peloton has been able to scale exercise, charismatic trainers, and community through video and Wi-Fi/Bluetooth technology. While Peloton has struggled post COVID, their user base and community will ensure stability once again.

MIRROR

Mirror is a novel home-based exercise platform where the primary interface is an LCD mirror. Users can watch live video classes in the mirror while watching their own movements and monitoring their heart rate. The mirror with speakers costs $1,500, and the monthly subscription is $39. The main benefits are convenience and a minimum footprint.

Performance Devices

GARMIN

Garmin, a U.S. company, is a global positioning satellite device company, historically focused on U.S. military applications. During the mid-2000s, the company entered the sports device market, which includes heart rate monitoring, GPS, and activity tracking. Garmin is the market leader in running, cycling, and triathlete training.

SUUNTO

Suunto, a Finnish company, was formed in 1932 to provide compasses to the Finnish Army. In 1992, the company launched a wrist device that functioned as a compass, altimeter, and barometer. Heart rate tracking and fitness tracking were eventually added.

ONLINE/APPS

MAPMYFITNESS MapMyFitness was an early mover in mobile fitness mapping and community apps. The company was founded in 2005 and purchased by Under Armour in 2013.

STRAVA Founded in 2009, the cycling app Strava took mobile fitness mapping and community to the next level. It tracks users' (and their friends') rides and displays the times on a leaderboard. Popular routes have a KOM, or king of the mountain, a designation for the fastest performer. The app tracks heart rate, estimates users' power while cycling, and offers a "suffer score" based on heart rate performance. The gamification, training goals and plans, and community feel have driven this app's growth.

TRAININGPEAKS TrainingPeaks was an early mover in web-based training logs. Training plans from well-known running, cycling, and triathlete coaches were added to appeal to the hard-core endurance athletes.

Constraints

CONGESTED MARKET This highly competitive market creates the need for a well-tested, crystallized message and offer. However, fifteen years ago, the same could have been said; industry leaders SoulCycle, Peloton, and Strava were created at that time. It is critical to dial in the right combination of exercise type, community, technology, personalization, and charismatic instructors.

CAPITAL This segment is generally capital intensive, whether that means adding new locations, creating and inventorying new equipment, or developing complex mobile apps. Even pilot projects can be costly as long-term leases are required and product development expenses are high.

HABIT FORMING New concepts must be effective to make users create and maintain new habits. The eSports game *Fortnite* has been able to develop a user base of over 120 million in less than two years. Humans generally understand that exercise is very beneficial though a minority of the population does it consistently.

CONVENIENCE For now, overcoming this feature seems to have the most traction. The idea of fitness that is home-based but has a community feel has driven growth. Geographic expansion of in-person training is costly.

COST Widespread adoption of exercise will not happen until price points fall dramatically. Technology can drive down costs, but equipment purchases can be a significant barrier.

Opportunities

The industry is at an inflection point of change and opportunity. COVID-19 has dramatically accelerated the trend away from generic fitness gyms to those with specialization, a strong community connection, enhanced service, or remote offerings. The traditional gym-goer's mindset of what is convenient exercise has largely changed due to the pandemic. Lots of equipment is not necessarily needed. Community is. The large "big box" gym chains will consolidate into three to five price point offerings—like Planet Fitness—or high-end offerings like Lifetime Fitness, which are supported by corporate benefits. For entrepreneurship, the new winners will be those who really invest in community engagement and unique offerings. This trend was already happening but will accelerate. Phygital offerings—in person and digital combined—will become the norm. Users will want flexibility in how they consume the service.

COMMUNITY In many ways, exercise will evolve like the entertainment industry. The key trend is further segmentation and the creation of niches. Other forms of exercise may emerge along with a strong community component and a clear sense of identity. This segmentation will likely manifest itself in small studios—likely in California or large urban areas—developing their own tribes. Additional offerings, such as mental health support or social elements, will be included to enrich the experience and create further earnings for the proprietor. Strong relationships between trainers and users will be the cornerstone of success.

TECHNOLOGY Creating networks online has been the force multiplier to help create scale for Peloton, Zwift, and Mirror. The next wave of startups will likely utilize technology to cut costs. Currently, market leaders charge $1,500 to $3,000 for initial investment and a $39 monthly fee for live video, metrics, and community. Copycat offers are creating great price pressure. A race to the price bottom will not be a successful tactic as there are already a number of $0.99 workout apps. There are opportunities for new tracking devices though they will have to develop under the constraints of high development costs and integration with mobile phone operating systems. New app-only development seems limited unless paired with a device or affiliated with a brand or community. Livestreaming—which can create a sense of community in a virtual environment—will accelerate more quickly. The digital fitness movement will be supported by vast libraries of previously recorded content, which will be rated by users the way Amazon is.

FURTHER "NICHE-IZATION"   The current offerings will likely be further segmented. Newer trends include high-intensity interval training (HIIT), parkour, rowing, the treadmill comeback, aerial exercise, and circus arts. Additional services like nutritional and mental health counseling will likely be included. Online training in niche sports will flourish as long tail demand is satisfied.

Going forward, startups will need the right balance of personalization, community, convenience, celebrity training, and price point. Most likely, there will be a combination of online and in-person experience. High-quality video and in-person production will be key ingredients.

6

Fan Experience

Overview

Fan experience is a fairly new concept. Gone are the days of the fans just being happy with getting through the stadium gates or seeing a box score on the screen. The best understood element is the game-day experience. Most people think of seating, concessions, and perhaps other amenities. But team owners have come to realize that the fan experience is much broader; it starts with parking, entering the stadium, food and beverages, merchandising, halftime activities, alternative viewing areas, bathrooms, nonsporting activities, departing the stadium, and exiting the parking lot. That is the physical part.

Nowadays, there is also the digital part—buying tickets, player and team stats, video highlights, and both team and player social media. Short-form video—YouTube and TikTok—is being used to show behind-the-scenes pregame and postgame content. Increasingly, more attention is devoted to content surrounding the live events.

Teams are combining physical and digital to create a phigital experience. COVID-19 only accelerated the trend—paper tickets and game-day programs have largely disappeared. Concessions and ordering merchandise will move to mobile with express pickup or delivery for a fee. Parking assistance will likely move to mobile GPS apps to simplify parking payment and assign spaces for more orderly traffic flow. Logistics communications will likely move to text messaging or a dedicated mobile app.

A great deal of innovation is happening to enhance the fan experience. Competition from video games, streaming TV shows, and mega movie theaters have raised the bar. Sports broadcasters have had to up the ante as the sports content segment has become saturated and mobile apps offer real-time content. In an effort to improve, teams have mapped out the fan experience with all of the touch points between fans, staff, and technology.

The one-stop-shopping fan engagement mobile app has yet to go mainstream. Besides the aforementioned logistics, behind-the-scenes content and player storytelling will be different from what fans are watching on traditional media. These mobile apps will likely evolve to be gateways for in-person and virtual fans. Elements will include forums, chat rooms, interviews, and prizes for competitions. Augmented reality will likely be driven by faster chips and the cultural acceptance of Google Glass–like eyewear. Google was too early, but in time augmented reality will prove too attractive to the mainstream.

Brief History

Stadium historians often refer to a certain lineage:

- Panathenaic Stadium in Athens, Greece (566 BC)
- Crosley Field in Cincinnati, the first MLB stadium with lights for night games (1936)
- Astrodome in Houston, the first multipurpose and domed stadium (1965)
- Oriole Park at Camden Yards, the first "retro" park with modern amenities (1992)

Oriole Park was designed by HOK Sport with a great deal of influence from Pilot Field, a minor league park, in Buffalo, New York. Its magic was the retro feel of an old park but one with modern amenities to enhance the fan experience. Club seats and luxury boxes were a fairly new introduction, along with picnic tables above the bullpen. The baseball-only park was a break from the prevailing trend of combined baseball and football stadiums. It is estimated the design has influenced twenty-three other MLB baseball parks while also influencing NFL stadiums.

As for the NFL, AT&T Stadium has been home to the Dallas Cowboys since 2009. The Atlanta Falcons upped the ante with Mercedes-Benz Stadium in 2017. However, in 2020, the game-day experience has forever changed with Allegiant Stadium, home of the Las Vegas Raiders, and SoFi Stadium, home of the Los Angeles Rams and Chargers.

The PGA has been a trendsetter in creating luxury alternative viewing areas—high-end tents with technology and high-end food and beverage—to accommodate sponsors and VIPs. The 2022 World Cup featured high-end modular stadiums that could be disassembled and moved to other parts of the country. All these additional amenities allow for pricing segmentation and generate upsell opportunities to create curated experiences.

These innovations are also creating a new category of architects, designers, coders, engineers, and builders to create these incredible structures.

On the digital side of fan engagement, we are in the early days; its "history" is arguably less than five to ten years. While cable TV, large screens, and sound systems have been available for over twenty years for those who could afford it, the real breakthrough was being able to watch games on your smartphone from 2015 to 2020. In effect, you could take the game with you. This development was due to increasing chip processing speed and broadband because video takes a great deal of processing power given the huge amount of data needed. The quality of the video stream is still the top priority for fans.

Over that same time, social media came to the forefront; teams started engaging fans and fans started engaging each other. Like other categories, social media helps users self-identify in tribes and engage in those tribes. In many instances, social media is the best way to keep up with breaking sports news and what is on the cutting edge. For example, Twitter is the best way to keep abreast of developments in soccer analytics. Most team-to-fan marketing has moved to social media, both organic and paid.

Known as the second screen, watching a game and scrolling through social media or advanced metrics is the optimal viewing experience. According to Deloitte, 58 percent of Millennials surveyed use social media to get team and player updates while watching the game. In fact, more than 52 percent would be interested in using social media as the primary game-viewing platform.

Broadcasters have jumped on the fan enhancement bandwagon by offering additional stats and graphics. MLB launched StatCast so fans can better track pitches and batted-ball launch angles and home-run tracking. The LA Clippers, along with Second Spectrum, offer CourtVision, which provides different viewing modes with expected shooting percentages for the players as well as animations to emphasize relevant moments. Most sports offer different commentators or viewing angles for games. Well-known pro athletes are investing in minor league teams as well as cocreating content. For example, NFL star Marshawn Lynch invested in the second division soccer team Oakland Roots and made a viral video of himself playing soccer, getting frustrated, and picking up the ball and scoring like an American football game.

Movie stars, scripted series creators, and rappers are getting in on the action. Ryan Reynolds and Rob McElhenney bought a fifth division soccer team in Wales and produced a documentary, *Welcome to Wrexham*, about it. The fictional soccer player characters of Apple TV's *Ted Lasso* have been added to the FIFA 23 video game. The sports network Overtime is a Gen Z–focused enterprise that generates short-form video on social media with their 16–19-year-old pro basketball league and 7v7 low-contact football league. The viewing is optimized for short-form video first and in-person fans second.

Tech giants Amazon, Apple, and Google are getting into the broadcast rights auctions with the aim of creating fan-enhanced experiences in-game as well as docuseries to watch between games.

Enormous growth is likely in this digital segment. The primary limiters are chip processing speed and bandwidth, such as the rollout of 5G. Augmented reality—whether screen or glasses—will likely be more prevalent in the next three to five years while wide-scale virtual reality is further out.

Key Players

The key players in the ecosystem of fan engagement are illustrated in figure 6.1.

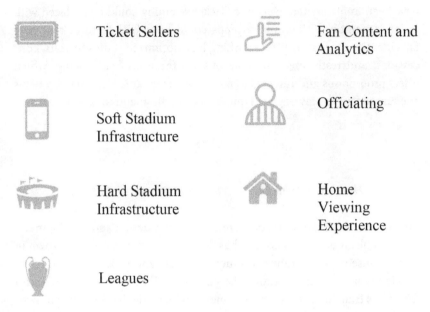

Ticket Sellers

Fan Content and Analytics

Soft Stadium Infrastructure

Officiating

Hard Stadium Infrastructure

Home Viewing Experience

Leagues

Figure 6.1.
Fan engagement ecosystem.

Ticket Sellers

Ticket purchases have moved largely online with Ticketmaster and team-owned ticketing websites such as Altitude Tickets. Ticket resellers have flourished with offerings from StubHub, VividSeats, and SeatGeek. Bundled offerings include concessions, current and retired player meet and greets, and VIP tours and parking.

Soft Stadium Infrastructure: Parking Attendants, Ticket Takers, Security, and Ushers

Often overlooked in the past, interactions with these staff members are usually the first points of contact. Depending on the organization, most staff are hired by the team. Customer service training and improved protocols have been implemented over time. Ticket scanning could be replaced with facial recognition. Mobile team apps could have GPS features that help fans identify the best available parking lots, optimized routes to seats, concessions, and restrooms. The GPS enables the use of geofencing, which offers promotions and rewards to fans in a certain area. This activity helps encourage fans to stay engaged outside the stadium and to return again.

Hard Stadium Infrastructure: Physical Assets

Tremendous innovation has occurred in stadium design and development. While public money for stadiums has declined, private money has grown in part because of the lucrative commercial, retail, and residential real estate development that occurs around the stadiums. While money is earned with the sports franchises, even more money can be made developing and owning the surrounding area.

The $1.6 billion Mercedes-Benz Stadium has an eight-panel retractable roof and a 360-degree Halo Display in the rafters. In addition to the retractable lower-bowl seating, the technology includes 2,500 TVs, 500 security cameras, approximately 4,000 speakers, 4,000 miles of fiber optic cable, 15,000 ethernet ports, 2,000 wireless access points, and 90 miles of audio cable. Concourses have areas that resemble sports bars, while entry and exit points are better designed to improve flow. Changes in concessions include mobile app ordering and food delivery to the seat, offering a variety of food and beverages while tracking consumer behavior. As most professional team stadiums are already built, the retrofitting of existing structures to new standards will likely create significant demand for innovation.

Leagues

The leagues have been thought leaders in getting teams to improve their fan experiences. Oftentimes, the leagues will do the early research on the technologies, set out an adoption roadmap, and share best practices with the team management.

Fan Content and Analytics

Marketing departments are doing a better job creating narratives around their teams, sharing origin stories and how the players overcome setbacks. These narratives include coaches and player interviews and specials. The teams are engaging fans before and after games in various polls and social media—Twitter, Facebook, Instagram, Snapchat, Reddit—while supporting official fan groups who have their own social media networks.

Sports fans are growing increasingly sophisticated in their knowledge of the game. The demand for real-time statistics and data visualization has grown with the "*Moneyball*-ization" of sports on both video screens and mobile apps. In-game prop bets—betting on what is going to happen on the next play—is becoming more of a reality as Wi-Fi and 5G wireless networks become more common. MLB and Apple partnered to create the At Bat app, where player pictures and stats will appear when users point an iPhone or iPad camera at the field.

In addition to measuring social media engagement, team marketing departments are analyzing GPS tracking and fan behavior and implementing loyalty programs and rewards to increase average fan purchases.

Players, teams, and third parties are experimenting with short-form video to tell stories in order to attract followers and increase engagement of their tribes.

Officiating

Officiating may be the next area for augmentation. In tennis, the Hawkeye system has served as an officiating resource since the early 2000s. In 2019, MLB evaluated computer umpires in the Atlantic League. In soccer, goal-line technology and video assist refereeing are being implemented globally across leagues. Using video analysis, referees evaluate contentious three-pointers and missed fouls.

Home Viewing

The home viewing experience is growing increasingly more sophisticated, particularly in a mobile environment. Sportscaster content has more analytics largely because the technology can support more real-time data and graphics are faster to produce. For some games, viewers can watch from multiple camera angles. Virtual and augmented reality choices are coming online.

The NHL was an early adopter of VR viewing of its 2016 All-Star Game. In 2017, NASCAR debuted a live, 360-degree pregame race through a phone, headset, or computer. Currently, 360 cameras are available in select driver cars during the races. Fox Sports, the broadcaster of NASCAR, has used Epic Games's Unreal Engine to create a virtual broadcast set where images are rendered to explain the races. The Golden State Warriors are deploying VR cameras so fans can watch the game with a 360-degree perspective. The NBA AR app allows fans to step inside a portal and look around 360 degrees behind the scenes during pre- and postgames. The BBC televised thirty-three men's 2018 World Cup soccer matches in VR. Liverpool Football Club is considering offering VR games to its worldwide fanbase as they already have difficulty accommodating 150,000 ticket applications for a stadium that holds 54,000.

ASO, the organizer of the Tour de France, works with Nippon Telegraph & Telephone (NTT) to track riders using GPS, which is relayed to the race media center for televised distribution and social media. NTT uses machine learning to predict outcomes given different peloton and breakaway configurations. In mountain bike racing, livestream videos from drone technology are making it possible for viewers to follow the race. Satellite GPS tracking allows fans to follow the Iditarod sled dog race in real time.

Constraints

NEED TO BUILD STUFF Most projects in this segment will likely need you to develop or retrofit buildings or create or implement technology hardware. For this reason, significant capital is needed.

STADIUM AND TEAM RELATIONSHIPS Long-standing relationships and track records are needed given the scale of the projects.

BUY-IN OF TEAM MANAGEMENT FOR MOBILE OFFERINGS You will have to get the team management on board for any mobile apps. While their endorsement will be huge, it will cost you. In time, leagues will likely look to sign deals with large, established mobile app players to designate an official league partner and share in the revenue.

Opportunities

This segment offers so many pathways for a potential startup. Fan engagement is hard. However, COVID-19 has forced the quicker adoption of new technologies with reduced friction at the stadium. The digital revolution is happening now. Increased fan engagement through mobile apps is going more mainstream as app developers upgrade their clunky first and second offerings. Data collection on fan behavior will be a huge opportunity for those who can collect information and convert it to improved workflow recommendations. Moreover, fans are becoming more comfortable with mobile community engagement and video storytelling. Traditional stadium upgrades are a huge opportunity if you have the construction experience, capital, and network.

RETROFITTING There will be ample opportunities for the installation of fiber optic cables, Wi-Fi access points, video screens, security video systems, and concourse redesign.

ANALYTICS Key areas include data collection through video or unique sensors, novel algorithms, and data visualization to better understand potential outcomes. While there are limited possibilities in large professional sports, niche sports likely offer more opportunities. Moreover, fan behavior data collection and analysis will be a huge opportunity to monetize.

FAN RELATIONSHIP MANAGEMENT Opportunities exist for tools that can simplify or improve the game experience. These include GPS-enabled navigation apps for fans and teams to track consumer behavior. Other tools could include data or platforms to help teams and players more easily engage fans. There could also be opportunities to develop best practices for training ticketing and stadium staff.

NEXT GENERATION ENTERTAINMENT Short-form video will drive entertainment between the games. The medium is perfect for sharing narratives and numbers. Content creators—teams, players, or independents—can greatly enrich the sporting experience. Sport and entertainment will continue to converge as players and entertainers benefit from shared experiences and cobranding.

In the medium term, there are tremendous possibilities in developing AR/VR game experiences, particularly with affordable and accessible VR engines such as Unreal Engine and Unity. These developments will greatly enhance fan experiences as well as athlete performance.

Personal Startup

I am a sports purist when it comes to watching games. But I would be a fool to focus only on purists in running a pro team. I'm that guy who would rather stay home and watch a game on TV so I can focus on the play without any distractions. I want to see the buildup and nuance with the help of a replay.

However, the days of focusing on the play on the field surrounded by spartan stands are long past. In the age of screens, it's hard for me to get through a ninety-minute soccer match where the ball is only in play for just less than an hour on average.

Two years ago, I went to a stadium that rather resembled an amusement park. I won't mention the team name as I don't want to offend my generous hosts. At first, I didn't like it. There were so many distractions—the game was also part light show and part music concert. It was hard to focus on the game. The seating area was a 40' x 60' patio where I could walk around and talk to different people sitting on outdoor furniture. Food and drink were everywhere. Massive screens replayed events and player profiles as the crowd roared. By the second half, I got more into the experience flow; in large part it was because everyone around me was having such a good time. I still saw the soccer purists, but they were standing by themselves drinking beer and focusing on the game.

Afterward, someone asked me what I thought of the game's quality of play. I honestly could not answer as I did not see enough of it to make an assessment. But it was a lot of fun. It was an immersive entertainment experience rather than watching a sports event. The light bulb went on for me.

So I went down a rabbit hole of immersive sports entertainment experiences. The NBA and NFL have been doing versions of entertainment for some time. But minor league sports are stuck in a time warp largely because they don't have the funds to create these experiences.

The incredible success of sports documentaries really hit the mainstream with ESPN's *30 for 30* series, gained steam in Amazon Prime's *All or Nothing* series and Netflix's *Drive to Survive*, and blew up with Netflix's *The Last Dance*. Sports stars and teams posting on social media created a new digital category of fan engagement. I came to the following conclusion.

Immersive game experiences are an absolute necessity where the non-sport components are as important as, if not more important than, the game. To double down, the content generated between the live games will be as important, if not more, for creating lasting team communities. The top five sports can count on ESPN, FoxSports, and others to keep the narrative going between games. But minor league teams will have to create their own content and distribution between games.

As a result, here is our playbook for Wilmington, though we realize only a few of these initiatives are going to land the first time. We will have to get the reps done in order to dial in the service.

Before we even schedule our first game, we will create a closed social network with threaded messaging and forums. We want to have a platform where we can communicate directly with our fans. This invite-only network will help us understand the different fan profiles and what they want out of game days and in between games, as well as how to create a Wilmington soccer lifestyle. In addition, we will look to draw non-soccer fans to understand how we can create an experience worth paying for and attending. These segments could include folks who appreciate local artists, foodies, and musicians. Before we do anything, we want to understand our community and how we can enhance their experience. We think that surveys—numbers and opinions—along with unstructured feedback will quickly help us map out the reality. We want to create a community that values soccer, art, music, food, and beer. The closed social network is a way to have thoughtful conversations about what community members really value.

Community input will greatly influence the design of our logo, uniforms, merchandise, and game-day experience. Below I have listed other areas we will explore:

- Public-facing social media for awareness and a call to action
- Ticket purchasing process
- A smooth parking experience
- Security and ticket scanning
- Finding seats and bathrooms
- Seating for different segments—VIP to cheap seats
- Ordering food on phone for pickup or delivery to seat
- Purchasing merchandise
- Halftime activities including on- and off-field entertainment, including play areas
- In-game music and fan group support
- Scoreboard content
- Departing venue

We want to make the most of the fifteen home-game experiences each year. As for the in-between game experiences, we will likely pilot the following:

- Documentary on the team startup
- Interviews with players and coaches
- Pregame and postgame podcasts or videos
- Storytelling training for pro players and staff, particularly in social media to better engage with fans

There are 350 days of the year without a soccer home-game experience. Our main community building block will be the food hall and beer garden. We will likely pilot the following:

- Weekly artist shows with a permanent outdoor gallery
- Weekly music concerts

- Foodie events and farmer's market
- Outdoor films
- Small-sided youth and adult leagues
- Auto and boat shows and faith events

Our goal is for the outdoor events center (the stadium) to become an important focal point for the community.

Interview

Nik Bonaddio—BigBrain
New York, NY
At first glance, Nik Bonaddio ticks all the boxes for a thought leader in analytics and fan engagement: computer science background, huge sports fan, and startup experience. He is wickedly smart and funny though he seems to know his own limitations and biases. He is a rare breed in that he was both a successful designer and developer.

Strange serendipity also played a huge role in numberFire, one company he founded, and later as chief product officer for FanDuel. Timing really mattered as the trend became his friend. Nik's input was instrumental as he developed the right networks in the media and with savvy investors. His mindset and process are precursors of the validation method explained later in the book.

CHRIS: Nik, tell us about yourself.
NIK: I grew up in Pittsburgh, a huge sports town, with the Steelers, Penguins, and Pirates. In the 1980s, there were so many sports superstars like Barry Bonds in Pittsburgh. I grew up middle class with a dad who was an engineer and a mom who was a homemaker. I earned a bachelor's and master's in computer science from Carnegie Mellon. I only really wanted to do two jobs ever. One was a stockbroker after I saw the movie *Wall Street*. But then, the internet happened in the mid-1990s. I decided what I wanted to do: sports and technology.

During those days, the lack of quality data was what drove me crazy in sports reporting. If you watched ESPN or read an article, there's so much qualitative conversation around sports. Everyone's talking about what might happen next or what the impact of some news might be. I saw a big gap in information you would expect from a trained scientist or engineer type. Sports are the most meticulously tracked. Every event has a final number: goals, touchdowns, or passing yards. Many assume that sporting events that happen over forty matches are completely random. During the mid-1990s to the mid-2000s, the Big Data revolution was happening in other industries because of massively increased processing power combined with large datasets.

Getting answers to hard questions became possible. What players should a team buy to win a championship? What player should I start on my fantasy team? How much is this player worth? A broadcaster could provide this evidence-based storytelling to inform and entertain their audiences. That's the career I wanted.

CHRIS: How do you think participating in sports at the collegiate level affected your view of sports analytics?

NIK: I've played sports all my life. In high school, I played tennis, soccer, football, and hockey. The playing experience gave me a start point and context to test variables and models of understanding. On the negative side, the experiences can also potentially narrow your thinking because you tend to assume certain things based on your own experiences, which may or may not be true. It's a gift and a curse. But team sports participation teaches a lot about leadership, competitiveness, ambition, and driving toward outcomes. When starting my company, all of the leadership and teamwork that I got from playing team sports helped me to run it more effectively.

CHRIS: You seem to have had this meteoric rise. You were at Yahoo! and two other startups before starting your own business. It is a mythological startup story, even though most evidence supports that the best age to start a business is in your mid-forties when you have networks and capital. How did your experiences at Yahoo! and your other startups inform your shift into your own business?

NIK: Yahoo! was my first job right out of college. I moved out to Silicon Valley to get a taste of the tech world. After a couple of years, I realized that a big company wasn't really right for me. I wasn't suited for the level of bureaucracy and slowness. Working at the other startups gave me a sense of the pace and how you solve problems. At a company like Yahoo!, everyone's got a very specific role, like a software engineer or a UX designer with a very specific task. In a startup, we need to hire

people with very flexible skill sets. Everyone is sort of broadly respon-
sible for product management and project management. The experiences gave me an idea of how to run things organizationally.

CHRIS: Data science has evolved quite a bit really since the 2000s. What did you
learn when you were at Carnegie Mellon? The revolution was happening.

NIK: That's right. Carnegie Mellon is famously a tech-oriented school. My
wife—who also went to CMU—and I joke about English and history
classes taught in a very sort of quantitative and logical way. We were
taught not to just assume things are the way they are. We were always
searching for more optimal, more efficient solutions. Many of my computer science classes weren't about the exact right way to code. The
professors cared about the way you went about the project and how
efficient the end process was. The mindset really helped me because
it taught me to reject conventional thinking analytics and predictive
technologies.

When I watched ESPN's *Pardon the Interruption*, they would give
all these opinions, none of which were grounded in data. That was the
gap I wanted to fill with numberFire. My startup experiences grounded
me in that one failed and the other was meandering along. I didn't have
the capital until my experience on *Who Wants to Be a Millionaire*.

CHRIS: Can you talk about this experience?

NIK: Yeah, I always used to read the Pittsburgh *Post-Gazette* to stay close to
what's happening at home. One day, there was an article that described
how *Who Wants to Be a Millionaire* was coming back for a tenth anni-
versary special. As I was pretty good with trivia, I called the number
to audition. It was a touchtone phone quiz. I answered five questions.
Nine months later, I'm sitting at my job and get a call saying that I've
been selected to be on the show. Regis was super friendly. Long story
short, I did well enough to make $100,000. My family wanted to move
back to Pittsburgh and buy a home as they are very conservative. After
paying the taxes, I basically quit my job the next day and started the
company. I thought winning on this game show was the equivalent of
walking down the street and finding a sack of money. So it was ser-
endipitous. It would have been foolish not to do something to invest
in myself.

You don't just start a data company. I can't just go and launch a
product. I had to collect data, build models, design prototypes, and
code. It took me a good year before I built something that I was comfortable showing to people. The data had to lead to useful insights.

It was a lot of work and super stressful. But it was actually one of the most fun working experiences because I'm driving toward this thing that I've had in my head. I had a binary mindset. Now, it is nothing. But the perfect outcome was in my head. Every day, I got up and chipped away at it. It was a long slog, but it was great.

CHRIS: I can't help being struck by the fact that good designers and good coders are not generally the same person. But it sounds like by necessity you had to be both.

NIK: I actually remember this very distinctly. In 1994, I was at Borders bookstore in Pittsburgh, and I picked up an HTML coding book. I was always into the internet before I knew what it could be.

I'd built many versions of personal websites because it was a really cool, unstructured canvas to design. I have always been a mix of designer and developer. CMU is actually a great school because it has a very strong design department. I was lucky enough to be able to major in computer science while taking many graphic design and communications classes. I learned a lot about color, gradients, and typography. I'm not a world-class designer, but I can create prototypes to test.

CHRIS: Your story is the proto-mythical story, namely about a sports/internet entrepreneur. A hero story. It's really the startup myth. We tell our students, wait a minute, this is not how it's actually done. It's fascinating to meet somebody who actually did it in that way with game show money to fund the early stages.

NIK: If it wasn't for *Who Wants to Be a Millionaire*, I don't know if I'd be talking to you now. I would just be an engineer at Google. I had a lot of things break my way. I obviously worked very hard. That's why I like talking to you, and I like working with other entrepreneurs. There's a survivor bias in startups; there are millions of startups that no one's ever heard of because they didn't make it. I had a lot of serendipity work my way and lots of helpful mentors. I do like to pay it back as much as I can. Startups are so romanticized, but they are very, very difficult.

CHRIS: I do think that luck is the most important thing in startups and in life. You just have to work really hard and be really smart to be prepared to be at the right place at the right time.

NIK: Luck happens. But luck happens more to people who work themselves to a place of preparedness.

CHRIS: The golfer Gary Player used to say, "The harder I work, the luckier I get." Let's talk about your transition from solopreneur to more. At some point, you are starting to get traction. Tell me about that inflection point. Then tell me about the one or two potential setbacks that could have just taken everything off the rails.

NIK: I launched the beta somewhere around the 2012 NFL season. I was connected relatively well in the startup world to get in front of some relatively influential people. During the first season, we got around 100,000 unique visitors and 50,000–60,000 registered users. I felt like there was something there. I knew enough about the marketplace as a big fantasy sports guy myself to know that it was differentiated enough. We got some good traction. I had to decide if this was just a hobby for me. Or can this be more? I never really thought about how to monetize the work because I was first more concerned with validating the demand. Was there a path to an actual business?

I joined a program called Insights, which matched entrepreneurs with MBA students from NYU and Columbia to get more business thinking around early-stage ideas. It was super helpful to talk about different business models. I went to the TechCrunch Disrupt conference, where I met five or six venture capitalists. But people weren't throwing money at me. The key takeaway was that there's something here. I needed a team to really scale the idea. We were too early to raise funds.

The middle ground was to join an accelerator called Era in New York. In exchange for equity, we got $25,000 if we completed the program. I got clarity on the business and really understood the unit economics, namely at the consumer level.

Most importantly, thirty to forty investors visited every week. The program really helped me build my network. By the time of the demo day, I already had a couple of checks confirmed. It was a springboard to raise my first financing round of $750,000 in 2013. I could hire a couple of people, get an office, and do it full-time. I think a lot of companies fall apart right around that stage, between the idea stage and scaling it into something that's more viable. I couldn't have done the scaling that I did unless I raised the financing.

Network and capital are very important. If I didn't have all those venture capitalists coming to see me at the accelerator program, I probably wouldn't have been able to raise the cash. Hiring right is another major driver. I was lucky enough to meet some really great hires. I had to sell them on the vision and the upside of what I was doing. The business jump-started and scaled to fifteen or so employees. We sold the company in 2015 to FanDuel when our revenue was about $2 million. We were able to develop a business where the unit economics were strong. I knew the business was sustainable, but I didn't know how to get to $10–20 million. When I was inside of FanDuel, I saw a company that would really super-power the intellectual property that we built. We knew that the IP was most valuable, but we needed more users to access inside of the FanDuel home. That's why we decided to sell the company.

CHRIS: It makes total sense. Acquiring those customers yourself would have been pretty costly. Better to merge for more distribution and customer acquisition.

NIK: In the beginning, we were one of a kind other than some more traditional scores and basic statistics. We were forging a new market. Over time, we saw more competitors coming up. There was a relatively fixed market size and new competition. It was getting more difficult. We saw some writing on the wall when ESPN hired a bunch of analytics people. We were still ahead of the curve as we were working on predictive analytics.

CHRIS: I want to focus on the $0–2 million revenue stage. There are a lot of wrecked startups there. What were the inflection points?

NIK: I never really thought of us as a media company. But many of our investors came from media backgrounds. Our lead investor was from RV Ventures, which is famous for investing in BuzzFeed, *Business Insider*, and other media investments. At first, I never really understood why we fit into their thesis. But the data itself is content.

They correctly understood that people did not want just numbers in giant PDFs. I had to figure out a way to editorialize that content. Based on their input, we started to write 100–200 articles weekly. We became a media company with data as the hook infused with humor. That was how we expanded our audience exponentially. I also realized that our offer was predictive enough in the fantasy space that customers were using it to handicap sports betting. I wanted to figure out how to get a cut of that business. We ended up using the content as a customer acquisition method for a subscription business with tools that helped people make better decisions in fantasy sports and sports betting.

Content became a giant acquisition tool. With one piece of content, you share on Facebook, Twitter, and emails. The effort brought people to our site, where you upsell them on the subscription tools.

In the media marketplace, the hardest-hit companies are the ones that strictly monetize via advertising. It is a very difficult business model.

But there are better ways to monetize. In our case, it was software subscriptions. In other cases, ecommerce could be the ticket. We pivoted to the secondary business model around subscription-based tooling. Software-as-a-service (SAAS) companies are the strongest companies, like Zoom and Slack. We built out a very nice business model that got us to $2 million in sales. That distilled two insights. One, it was understanding the business as a media company and not a data company. Two, we moved to a SAAS model with content and data as our hooks.

CHRIS: So, statistics alone is not enough. You've got to wrap a narrative around data to get the eyeballs. A subscription-based model is the most sustainable way of scaling.

NIK: As a designer, I don't want to have a bunch of ads on my site. I thought that I could build tools to allow people to adjust a couple of variables, like rushing yards but not passing yards. The users can explore and filter the data on their own terms. These tools empower the end user to develop the insights that they want. I knew that my target audience was similar to my friends and me. I'm the prototypical end user for the product. It wasn't hard to think about what features we should build because it was intuitive.

CHRIS: How have all these experiences influenced what you're doing to FanDuel?

NIK: I have been a huge fan of FanDuel. In the beginning, I was shepherding numberFire into the FanDuel system. The logic was that our underlying analytics supports many of the back-end processes at Fanduel. We started in daily fantasy sports and then expanded into sports betting. Like numberFire, FanDuel was scaling quickly in this new frontier. I wanted to help infuse entrepreneurial thinking into the larger organization. As I was running the product team, I had the best of both worlds. I could be very entrepreneurial by quickly developing new ideas. The organization's scale provided safety nets. Many founders leave quickly after their companies are sold in part because of the cultural change. It's not a surprise to say that I'm going to start another company at some point, as that is who I am. I was a kid with a lemonade stand and then selling baseball cards.

CHRIS: Where do you see the opportunities going forward?

NIK: The big opportunity is helping organizations understand how to use the data and translate it into actions. You would be surprised at how many large professional sports organizations don't know how to use the data. The field is open in college sports and below though it may take more time to evolve. The data needs to be editorialized along with a toolkit so teams can create actionable outcomes.

Forward-thinking organizations will use analytics to better engage their fans via social media. They will be able to explain the goal and the thinking behind it. Data can manifest itself in so many different parts of your organization.

I usually start with determining the size of the total addressable market. I see lots of companies focusing on the relatively small market size of sports team organizations with bigger wallets versus fewer organizations focusing on a much larger market of consumers with smaller wallets. Let's talk to these consumers about their pain points so we can build tools to solve their problems. On the consumer side, fantasy sports was the biggest opportunity. There is less competition in the consumer space.

I see some opportunities in the B2B space. It's limited in that there are about 120 teams in the big professional sports and 200 Division 1 college teams. However, there are hundreds of millions of sports fans. I am a proponent of always going after the bigger market even though the pocketbooks will be smaller.

Many companies expect the U.S. sports betting market to evolve just like the markets did in Europe. I fundamentally think that's incorrect. Fantasy sports have been a part of the sporting life. People tend to think of things in terms of how players are going to do when they think about how teams overall are going to do. There are opportunities to break things down on a player level versus a team level. We have to wrap the analysis into a complete experience with tools and relevant content, which are tied into podcasts. How do you give people the confidence that they've got an inside track on things? That's how you create a powerful acquisition engine through content.

FanDuel and DraftKings are making investments in the analytics and content space. More companies are offering free-to-play games and content as the hook. I think streaming games in your app will become really important. It probably won't happen with the NFL as it's cost prohibitive. I could see it happening in tennis and soccer. It's almost a gold rush. The first mover advantage is so important as each state opens to sports betting. But over time, the better product will win as the offer will distill down to what the user really cares about in betting. Special promotions may work now. Later it will mature to how easy it is to deposit, withdraw, or find the content that they want now. It's all about user experience.

Online dating apps are perfect examples. The segment evolved from eHarmony to Match to OkCupid to Tinder. As each iteration happened, the feature sets of the various apps got more specific and more experience based. I see sports betting evolving the same way. The products will narrow down to a smaller set of functionalities and experiences. I'm not worried about traditional players like Caesars and MGM. I'm really worried about three frat boys at Stanford who look at our app and say that this is the way my dad does it; this isn't the way that I want to do it. We have to be constantly ready to rethink the way that users interact with these apps.

CHRIS: The dating app market comparison is perfect. However, there is significant protection in that the sports betting markets are heavily regulated and require lots of capital, so the kids won't be starting sportsbooks. But new startups can nibble away the value of the related businesses of handicapping or helping people make their bets.

NIK: It drives me crazy that the old-school touts and handicappers are making recommendations not grounded in data science. The segment is starting to professionalize. Sportsbooks are developing relationships with folks at MIT or CMU to treat data science the same way Wall Street treats data science. This knowledge will slowly trickle down to the everyday consumer. There's a large company to be built around that demand, probably as a subscription model.

CHRIS: What do you think about the evolving concept of data rights as it relates to image rights?

NIK: If I owned a team, I would collect my own data and have an API for anyone willing to pay a subscription. I want other people doing things with my IP because it only provides more value back to me. I would host hackathons to engage with the developer community. They would help me learn how to change the stadium experience and engage with fans over the next five to ten years. It is going to have a natural advantage over other legacy companies that don't really approach data the same way. Yes, competitors will get the info, but the benefits would more than outweigh the disadvantages. Keeping information in an ivory tower stifles innovation.

Facebook supercharged its growth when it opened up its platform. Developers can build games inside of Facebook. I believe very strongly that there's a correlation between openness and people building things on top of your system that ultimately drives value back to you.

CHRIS: What advice would you give to your younger self?

NIK: I made mistakes, but I was lucky enough to have found my way. I don't have any regrets. In the early stages of a startup, you have to manage your mental health from therapy to talking regularly with friends. You have to believe in yourself and keep fighting. I found that when it was really hard. I reminded myself that someone else had to overcome a similar problem. Don't be afraid to ask for help, especially in having a mentor. I think a healthy lifestyle really matters. That means plenty of sleep. Things will always take longer. Think of the startup experience as more of a marathon than a sprint.

7

Discover

Going forward, we turn our attention to how to generate an idea and turn it into an enterprise. We will use the DIVA—discover, ideate, validate, and accelerate—method to make the process easy to understand. Let's recap each step before we deep dive into the process.

Discover

In the first stage, we evaluate how to align your daily efforts with your main goals. We inventory what you do and what you want to do. In short, we map your reality and sketch out alternative paths to success.

Ideate

We develop a process of creating and crystallizing ideas by developing user profiles and journeys. We map out current best practices and competitors.

Most importantly, we get user and stakeholder feedback to understand reality.

Validate

We create and iterate prototypes for users to find a balance between what users are willing to pay and what we can deliver profitably and sustainably.

Accelerate

Once we have a go, we focus on how to grow quickly with promotion and distribution, collateral development, sales management, scaling operations, managing and leading, budgeting, and fundraising.

Discover

Veronica thought she had it all figured out. With a master's in nursing, she had a great-paying job and fabulous kids, and she helped out at her father's church. Veronica had recently lost forty pounds and translated that intensity into helping others lose weight by starting a weight loss consultancy. She attended my workshops to translate her side hustle into a full-time business. She perfectly cleared her checklists weekly in an effort to start her own weight loss center. Veronica was both relentless and charmingly full of life.

I saw her several months later. She looked tired but still had the fire. Her business had scaled as she applied first-rate sales and marketing tactics to an untapped market. She told me that she had decided to get her PhD to add credibility to her business. I think that she also wanted the additional validation.

I ran into Veronica a year later. She was haggard and guarded. Being an entrepreneur, mother, wife, and student all at once had caught up to her. She felt that the walls were closing in. Previously, her drive for perfection was a key to success. Now, her drive was an unforgiving taskmaster. Her grades had slipped and she was forced to dial back on clients. Veronica felt guilty that she was not always able to be there for her family. She had gained weight and had no time for herself.

Veronica learned the brutal lesson: you can't have it all. You really can't. Success depends on making trade-offs on exciting competing options. Success depends on setting clear priorities and being relentless about the top priorities. It also means accepting and embracing that you will rarely get your checklist completely done.

Happiness is a function of shared, realizable expectations. Veronica went through a process of mapping out reality by how she spends a day. She wrote down her priorities and the identified gaps in how she spends the day relative to those priorities. Veronica slimmed her goals down to their essence.

Veronica fell into a startup's common trap. She underestimated the work needed to start up a business in the real world. The truth is that start-ups generally take twice as long and need twice as much capital as you think. The key action is to map out that reality, evaluate alternative scenarios, and answer one key question.

In these next four chapters, we will go through a process that will turn an idea into reality in as short a time as possible. The goal is to teach you the least you need to know to be successful. Entrepreneurs tend to be just-in-time learners and want to cut to the chase in as few words as possible. We have to first answer the question: Is the juice worth the squeeze?

Discover Toolkit

In this chapter, we ground you in your current reality by comparing how you spend your waking hours with your goals. We examine different aspects of your life. Finally, we map out the different ways the future can unfold. The goal is to align your daily efforts to your main goals. This process will help you understand how much squeezing you have to do to get the juice. Here are the main tools:

- Reality Map
- Priority and Reality Alignment
- Personal Inventory Assessment (PIE)
- Alternative Path Sketch

Several tools are inspired by thoughtful concepts in Bill Burnett and Dave Evans's outstanding book, *Designing Your Life*. A free Google spread-sheet toolkit template is available on the sports entrepreneur website.

Reality Map

Let's start at square one. How do you currently spend your time? Estimate that you have fifteen available hours daily or one hundred hours weekly. Assume that you spend nine hours each day sleeping, getting ready for bed in the evenings, and preparing for work or school in the mornings. During the course of the week, how much time do you spend at work or school, on family time, and on entertainment and screen time? Guesstimate these times using the following chart (see figure 7.1). Modify it to fit your needs. Create a graph. A daily guesstimate may be the easiest place to start. Check your smartphone to see how many hours you spend on the screen. Then track your actual hours over the next one or two weeks. How does reality compare to your guesstimate?

Next, let's categorize activities based on how much you like doing them. The goal is simple to understand but difficult to do. Do those things you enjoy more. Only do those things you don't enjoy if they are worth the squeeze.

Attention	Satisfy	Energizing	Activity
5	4	4	Work/School
4	5	4	Exercise
3	3	2	Screen time/Entertainment
5	3	3	Family time
3	4	3	Socializing
3	3	3	Social Media
2	2	2	Transit
2	2	2	New Projects
2	2	2	Other

Target Waking Hours: 100 = (15 hours awake X 7 days) - 12 hours eating. Change if you want.

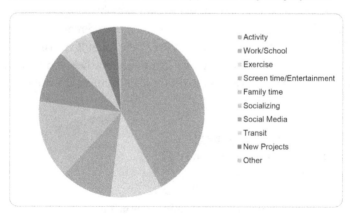

Figure 7.1.
Mapping your reality.

Using a scale of 1–5, rate the activity based on focus, satisfaction, and energizing.

Focus: Rate it from 1, for little attention needed, to 5, which requires your full attention.

Satisfaction: Rate it from 1, for joyless, to 5, which is so joyful that you forget about time.

Energizing: Rate it from 1, for joyless, to 5, which is so joyful that you forget about time.

Let's rework the activities in figure 7.2. List the activities that you find energizing, draining, requiring attention, and satisfying.

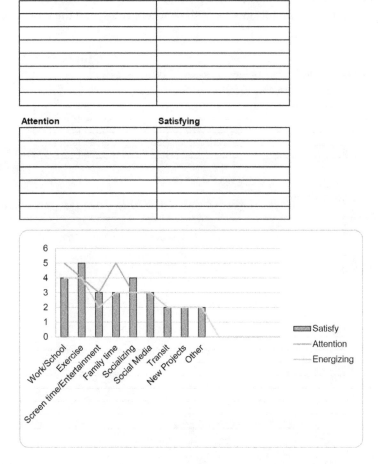

Figure 7.2.
Activities categories.

Take a long look. Schedule more time to do the things in which you forget about time. Get rid of the activities that are draining or not satisfying if they are not helping you achieve a larger goal. Balance activities that require lots of focus with things that do not (listening to the radio and completing expense reports).

Priority and Reality Alignment

Let's turn our attention to the priorities and how you value them. Start out general and get specific.

List out the following activities: Work/School, Play, Relationships, Explore New Things, and Health (see figure 7.3). Rank them from most important to least important. Next, show where you spend the most effort:

KEY AREAS RANKING Rank from highest (1) to lowest (5)	Priority (1–5)	Reality (1–5)	Difference P-R	Satisfy (1–5)	P-S
Explore New Things			0		0
Health			0		0
Play			0		0
Relationships			0		0
Work/School			0		0

Complete after other sections
GENERAL CONCLUSIONS
Description

Goals/Next Steps

Figure 7.3.
Activities ranking template.

1 is the most and 5 is the least. Finally, list them from the most satisfying to the least satisfying. Have a look at the differences.

In each section (see figure 7.4), write a brief summary of each of the activities: Work/School, Play, Relationships, Explore New Things, and Health. Write out goals and next steps to align your priorities and reality.

Write short paragraphs describing priorities, realities, and next steps/goals with dates.

WORK/SCHOOL

Description

RELATIONSHIPS

Description

Goals/Next Steps

Goals/Next Steps

Break down into categories if applicable

PLAY

Description

HEALTH

Description

Goals/Next Steps

Goals/Next Steps

Figure 7.4.
Activities summary template.

Personal Inventory Assessment

In this section, you will do a deep dive on your life, work, school, and startup. You will rate key metrics on how important they are to you as well as how well you are currently achieving them.

LIFE

In each of these categories, rate from 1–5 how important they are to you in the goals column and how well you are achieving them in the reality column.

Family: How are your relationships?
Connected: Do you feel connected to others outside of family?
Money: Are you generating income to sustain your lifestyle?
Spiritual: Are these needs being met?
Work: Is the subject interesting and the environment positive?
Development: Do you have the opportunity to improve?

In the template (see figure 7.5), the radar charts are automatically generated. Identify the gaps and write down how you can reduce those gaps.

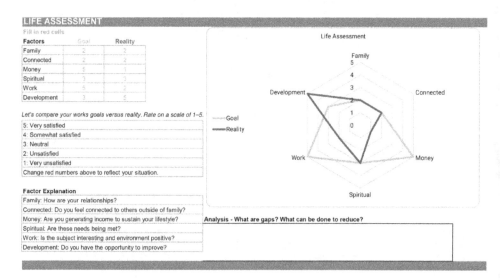

Figure 7.5.
Life assessment template.

WORK

In each of these categories, rate from 1–5 how important they are to you in the goals column and how well you are achieving them in the reality column. If you are a student, skip to the next section.

Interesting: Do you find the work interesting?

Money: Are you able to make ends meet?

Recognition: Do you get acknowledged by peers and superiors?

Growth: Do you feel that you are developing?

Connection: Are you able to develop meaningful professional relationships?

Helps Others: Are you able to assist others?

In the template (see figure 7.6), the radar charts are automatically generated. Identify the gaps and write down how you can reduce those gaps.

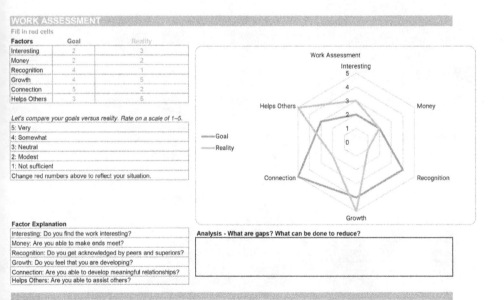

Figure 7.6.
Work assessment template.

SCHOOL

Complete this section if you are a student.

In each of these categories, rate from 1–5 how important they are to you in the goals column and how well you are achieving them in the reality column.

Interesting: Do you find the learning interesting?
Recognition: Do you get acknowledged by peers and professors?
Growth: Do you feel that you are developing?
Connection: Are you able to develop meaningful relationships?
Helps Others: Are you able to assist others?

In the template (see figure 7.7), the radar charts are automatically generated. Identify the gaps and write down how you can reduce those gaps.

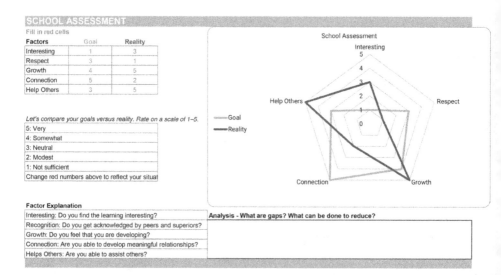

Figure 7.7.
School assessment template.

STARTUP/BUSINESS

Complete this section if you have a startup in mind or if you have an established business.

In each of these categories, rate from 1–5 how important they are to you in the goals column and how well you are able to achieve them in the reality column.

Passion: How strongly do you feel about the project?
Industry Knowledge: Do you have expertise in the project area?
Business Skills: Do you have the business skills to execute it?
Network: Do you have the necessary contacts to make the project work?
Sustainable: Can the project generate positive cash flow within 24 months?
Fundable: Can startup funds be raised for this project?

In the template (see figure 7.8), the radar charts are automatically generated. Identify the gaps and write down how you can reduce

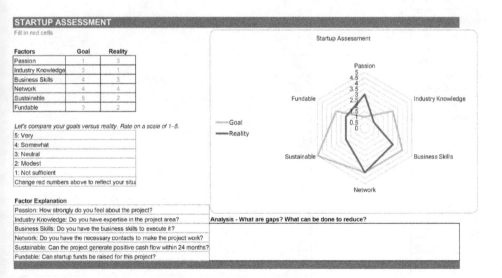

Figure 7.8.
Startup assessment template.

those gaps. Consider finding partners who are strong in the areas in which you need help. Generally, you don't want to start up a business if you have 3 or below in these categories. Keep in mind that a strong network can help overcome shortcomings in industry knowledge or business skills.

Alternative Path Sketch

In this section, we map out different life paths (see figure 7.9). The goal is to help you understand key events during your next two years. We also map out a scenario where things go badly in the next seven to twelve months and consider how you would respond. Finally, we think through what you

LIFE PATH MAPPING

Fill out time line below to include work, trips, health goals and significant events

Path #1		0–6 months	7–12 months	13–18 months	19–24 months
Current Plan!					
Gauge (1 to 5)					
Passion?					
Resources?					
Network?					
Confidence?					
Consistent?					

Path #2		0–6 months	7–12 months	13–18 months	19–24 months
Something goes wrong...					
Gauge (1 to 5)					
Passion?					
Resources?					
Network?					
Confidence?					
Consistent?					

Path #3		0–6 months	7–12 months	13–18 months	19–24 months
If money didn't matter...					
Gauge (1 to 5)					
Passion?					
Resources?					
Network?					
Confidence?					
Consistent?					

Figure 7.9.
Life path mapping template.

would do if money was not an issue. This possibility serves as a marker on how you may want to change your life.

In Path #1, write out the likely key events—work, family, vacation, training, etc.—during the next two years in six-month intervals. Rate from 1–5 (with 5 being the best) how strong your passion, resources, confidence, and network would be. In addition, rate how this path is consistent with what you really want to do.

In Path #2, imagine that something goes wrong within the next twelve months. How can you pivot effectively? Write out the likely key events—work, family, vacation, training, etc.—during the next two years in six-month intervals. Rate from 1–5 (with 5 being the best) how strong your passion, resources, confidence, and network would be. In addition, rate how this path is consistent with what you really want to do.

In Path #3, write out the likely key events during the next two years if money didn't matter. Rate from 1–5 (with 5 being the best) how strong your passion, resources, confidence, and network would be. In addition, rate how this path is consistent with what you really want to do.

Conclusion

Is the juice worth the squeeze given where your priorities are and reality is?

Have a look at the charts that you created. Reflect on where the gaps are. Crystallize in your mind what the highest priorities are in your life, work, play, and relationships. Develop a consistent narrative of what needs to be done to achieve your goals.

What We Covered

1. Main topic: Is the juice worth the squeeze?
2. We learned how to use the following tools:
   a. Reality Map
   b. Priority and Reality Alignment
   c. Alternative Path Sketch

8

Ideate

Ideate

Good ideas are nearly impossible to think up out of the blue. The reality is that all the easy ideas have already been thought up. At this point, you need to have subject matter expertise and a unique angle of approach. When you think up an idea, do a Google search. More than likely, you will find something similar. The most common innovation is to create a new way of doing an existing thing.

Here is an example. As you know, I am a sports fan. I am fascinated with evaluating sports in different ways: video, analytics, physiology, and sports psychology. In 2004, I took a year off to write a novel and enjoy the first year of having a child. I was a big baseball fan. That year, I decided to do a deep dive on sabermetrics—alternative metrics for baseball—and the core content in the book *Moneyball*. While at times, I would get lost in the math, I really enjoyed the approach. Over the years, I bought Baseball Prospectus and the equivalent preseason guides in other sports including Warren Sharpe's football and Richard Lu's basketball guides. I did not find anything for soccer.

In 2020, during COVID-19, I had the good luck of meeting Chris Darwen, the founder of *Total Football Analysis* magazine. The European media company offered weekly soccer analytics for many different leagues around the world. At the end of a long conversation, I pitched the idea of doing soccer preseason guides for the Premier League. Within ninety days, we launched our first guides, which were sold globally on Amazon in hard copy and eBook.

Ideas turn into reality most quickly when you have subject matter expertise, a solid network, and an innovation process. And money. But you need less capital if you have more expertise and a better network.

Developing subject matter expertise is not hard in our era, particularly not the segments in this book. The reason is that most segments are fairly new, so it is easy to get up to speed. In most areas, you can become subject matter fluent after about twenty to forty hours of research. Spend forty-five minutes daily reading about or interviewing experts you find on the internet or LinkedIn. Becoming an expert may take years, but once fluent, you can partner with people who know things you don't know. You can also develop executional skills like website design, social media marketing, negotiating, and video and audio editing. Exercise patience when you do not have an idea. Develop your subject matter expertise, build out your network, and develop skills. The ideas will present themselves if you apply the innovation process.

The process will help you move through the following stages:

1. Unknown-unknown: You don't know what you don't know.
2. Known-unknown: You know what you don't know.
3. Known-known: You know what you know. Now you can start innovating.

The practical tools for idea generation are easy to follow. Keep a physical or digital notebook and track the following over time:

What Makes Me Frustrated List (WTF)

Keep a running tab on things that make you frustrated. What are the gaps that you see that are not being met?

Cool Products and Services

Track those things that make a big or little difference in your life. Give some thought to how you could apply versions of those things to sports to create an innovative idea.

User Research

Settle on a user group that you want to help. Ask them what their pain points are and what they would be willing to pay to eliminate them.

Idea Sketch

An idea sketch is a snapshot of the most important elements of your concept. The goal is to put all the data on one page to crystallize the concept into a specific idea. Give yourself no more than fifteen minutes to get it down. Don't be a perfectionist at this time; you will be testing your idea over time with real potential users.

Be specific even though you are guessing. It's better to be specific and wrong than fuzzy; it means you can pivot more quickly. Here are the key elements:

Product or Service Definition

Include what the product is and its main features. (<10 words)

Key Functional Benefit

Describe the main benefit that the product provides. (<10 words)

Key Emotional Benefit

People make decisions based on emotions and justify them later with select facts. Explain the emotional trigger that you are satisfying. (<10 words)

Users

Describe one or two potential users using several key adjectives. (<10 words)

Stakeholders

List any potential organizations that will impact the enterprise in terms of finding customers or providing products or services that you will need. (<10 words)

Competitors

List your competitors and what they are best at after a quick online search. (<10 words)

Expert Mentors

List some people you can call or meet with who can help you learn about the product, user, or ecosystem. (<10 words)

Constraints

List the main constraints. (<5 words each)

Questions

List any questions that you have. (<7 words each)

Ideas rarely come when you are trying to think of them. The workable ideas tend to accrete over time, especially when you share those ideas with experts in the field. Their input will likely save you a great deal of time and money.

User Profile

Let's dive deeper into your potential users and their experiences (see figure 8.1). Give the user a specific name. Imagine that you are describing a good friend.

List out the key demographic information: gender, age, income, education, etc.

Describe what they do for fun and what media they consume and their social media habits.

Create a psychographic profile of what motivates them.

Explain what need they are trying to solve with your product or service.

Be clear about the emotional need you are trying to solve.

Demographic

Describe basic user characteristics such as age, gender, income, education, etc.

Psychographic

Describe headspace by characterizing media consumed, lifestyle, and life philosophy

Unmet Need

10–12 word description

Potential Solutions

3–4 different solutions

Features

4–5 main features of service/product

Potential Key Benefit

2–3 potential key benefits to narrow down to one...

Figure 8.1.
User profile template.

User Journey

Map out the user experience by addressing the following questions:

1. How does the user become aware of the product or service?
2. How do they do research on the product or service?
3. How do they purchase or consume the product or service?
4. What happens if there is a problem?

A marketing and customer service plan can be created by answering the four questions in figure 8.2.

Awareness

How does user first become aware of service/product and see repeat images

Research

Describe how user researches the service/product (influencers, online, word of mouth, retail)

How and Where to Buy/Consume

Describe how and where user buys/consumes the service/product

Problem

What happens if there is a problem

Figure 8.2.
User journey template.

Ecosystem Map

Sketch out the ecosystem around your product or service (see figure 8.3). Draw a circle in the middle of a page and write in the user's name. Add other circles around it and include the names of key stakeholders—people or enterprises that could impact your business. Put the key competitors in boxes with lines connecting to the user. At the bottom, write down any constraints and the open questions that you have.

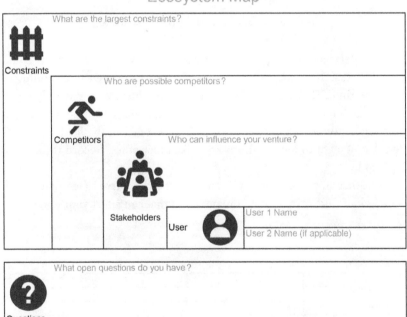

Figure 8.3.
Ecosystem map.

Best Practices and Features Comparison

Do an online search of who else is trying to solve the problem. Create a features comparison chart that includes competitor names on the y-axis while adding the key benefit, features, pricing structure, size, etc. on the x-axis (see figure 8.4). Fill in or check the boxes to complete the comparison. Search for gaps that other competitors do not offer. How will your offer be different from others? Do not be discouraged if competitors exist; they validate that there is market demand. Focus on how your offer will be different from theirs. Update the idea sketch and user profile and experience as needed.

Expert and Stakeholder Interviews

Expert interviews are a great way to get to reality quickly. Experts could include researchers, journalists, or people who have been in the industry for some time. These face-to-face or telephone interviews may only be an hour long, but the information learned can save you many hours of wasted time. Do an online and LinkedIn search for experts in the field. Prepare a tight list of eight to ten questions and take great notes. Record the session if possible.

Another important survey is the stakeholder survey (see figure 8.5). Stakeholders are anyone or an organization that can affect your enterprise:

	Enterprise	Competitor 1	Competitor 2	Competitor 3	Competitor 4
Feature 1					
Feature 2					
Feature 3					
Feature 4					
Feature 5					
Feature					

Figure 8.4.
Features comparison template.

How would you like to see the product/service improve?
What are your key constraints?
What are your key organization's needs?
What do you not like about current services/products?
What improvements do you suggest?
What are the key benefits that the user is seeking?
What is the primary market for this product/service?
What is the secondary market for this product/service?

Figure 8.5.
Stakeholders and experts question list.

suppliers, influencers, bloggers, etc. The survey questions may be similar to the user and expert interviews. The goal is to determine what needs they have that could positively affect your enterprise. Vendors will have minimum order quantities and lead times, influencers may want further recognition, and bloggers may want to have something new to tell their followers. These are important constraints to resolve when creating your service or product.

User Surveys

We have been able to make best guesses in the user profile and journey. The next step is to test using surveys—both online and in person; they are essential for gathering and organizing user feedback. The goals include identifying, categorizing, and prioritizing explicit and latent needs. Explicit needs are those where the user has a clear opinion. They choose an answer in a multiple-choice question or fill in what they would like to see in a product. Latent needs are those where the user cannot clearly express their opinion. Insights can be found by observing the user's body language or the way they answer the questions. Online surveys are great for reaching

How would you like to see the product/service improve?
What do you enjoy about current products?
What do you not like about current products?
What are your key issues when buying?
What improvements do you suggest?
What are the most important points we should understand?
Add demographic questions...
Remember
Position yourself as researcher rather than owner.
Clearly define the user.
Let go of preconceived notions.
Determine user priorities.
Be aware of latent needs.

Figure 8.6.
User questions list.

many potential users to identify explicit needs. In-person interviews, which are more open-ended in nature, are best for identifying latent needs. The interviewer can ideally give more latitude to the potential user.

It is often best to start with some online surveys to understand user needs and habits. Figure 8.6 includes some sample questions to consider. Feel free to copy, edit, and add questions as you see fit.

Opportunity Recognition Chart

After you have started to crystallize the opportunity, now it's time to do an initial check on how the needs map matches your skills and resources. Use the startup assessment radar chart in figure 8.7 to understand where you will need help. This step will be a quick check of whether the juice is worth the squeeze, and it will give you specific directions to get to a known-known status.

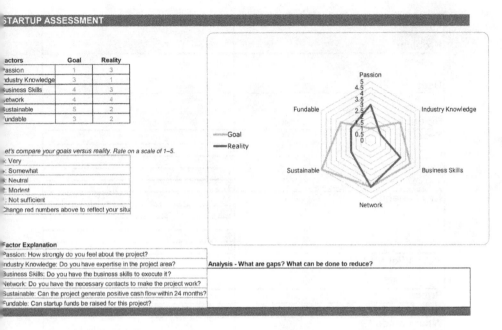

STARTUP ASSESSMENT

actors	Goal	Reality
'assion	1	3
ndustry Knowledge	3	1
3usiness Skills	4	3
Jetwork	4	4
3ustainable	5	2
'undable	3	2

et's compare your goals versus reality. Rate on a scale of 1–5.

3: Very
): Somewhat
1: Neutral
2: Modest
: Not sufficient

Change red numbers above to reflect your situa

Factor Explanation
Passion: How strongly do you feel about the project?
ndustry Knowledge: Do you have expertise in the project area?
Business Skills: Do you have the business skills to execute it?
Network: Do you have the necessary contacts to make the project work?
Sustainable: Can the project generate positive cash flow within 24 months?
Fundable: Can startup funds be raised for this project?

Analysis - What are gaps? What can be done to reduce?

Figure 8.7.
Startup assessment template redux.

With the exercises in this chapter, you are getting closer to moving from the unknown-unknown to the known-unknown to the known-known to reality. Note that what you think is reality may or may not be. The next step is to test—or validate—your hypothesis.

After completing these steps, be sure to update previous sections to create a consistent, clear viewpoint.

Service or Product Definition

Next, create a one-page summary that clearly describes the service or product (see figure 8.8). This summary represents what your best guess is in reality. This definition will serve as the starting point for you to create a prototype to test with users. It will likely evolve as you get more information from users and stakeholders.

Problem	
User	
Solution	
Features	1
	2
	3
	4
	5
Key benefits	1
	2
	3
	4
	5
How different?	
Price	
How to develop and cost?	
Where made?	
Next steps	1
	2
	3
	4
	5

Figure 8.8.
Service/product definition template.

Conclusion

In this chapter, we focused on finding the reality for your service or product. We crystallized our views of who the user is and what their wants are. We learned from experts. We identified what stakeholders need to support you. In short, we determined what the constraints are so we can design a solution made for reality.

9

Validate

Validate

Introduction

In the last chapter, we mapped out reality and identified gaps. We should feel that we are now on firm ground assuming that we were open to user and stakeholder feedback, know who our competitors are, and have done some best-practice analysis. You will have a much greater chance of success if you embrace the mindset of letting the user guide you and accepting the constraints for what they are. Don't get stuck on being right all the time. The next step is to answer these questions: Will users pay you enough to offer the product or service profitably? Can you find the right balance between user needs, profit, and your team's capability?

You need to create a low- or no-cost prototype to test. Based on the reality hypothesis, we will confirm viability with stakeholders and users by iterating a prototype with constant feedback.

Create Prototype and Wireframes

Based on the ideate process and survey, develop a physical prototype if it is a product or create a wireframe (or schematic) if it is a service. This iterative process entails creating a prototype, getting user and stakeholder feedback, and then revising the prototype.

Product

Create a prototype using low-cost materials. Don't overengineer the first version; the materials could be chicken wire and duct tape, the parts could just be glued together, or it could be a 3D-printed item. The key is to get a product into potential users and stakeholders' hands so they can give you feedback. Their suggestions will likely change the product requirements significantly. It's better to quickly make the prototype rather than be a perfectionist.

Service

Create a wireframe—a first version of what the website or app will look like. Sketch out the design on paper as a first version. Use prototyping software such as Adobe XD or Proto.io. You can learn the basics of these two software programs in less than an hour. In the prototyping software, potential users can click through the various links. Consider doing a web-based app instead of a mobile app as mobile app development starts at a minimum of $20,000 and can go upward of $100,000. The best practice is to start with a web app that evolves to a mobile app when you get traction. Get the prototype in front of potential users and stakeholders so they can give you feedback. Modify the wireframe and get more feedback.

Website

A website needs to be created for a product or service. Generally, it includes a homepage, a product or service offer page, an about us page, and a contact page. Easy-to-use web platforms include Squarespace and Wix. Shopify is a solid choice for e-commerce. Following is a summary of the key content and an example.

HOMEPAGE

1. Key benefit (< 8 words)
2. Visual or video that reinforces the key benefit
3. Product or service description (< 10 words)
4. Introductory video (< 90 seconds)
5. Introduction to product and business (< 100 words)
6. Validation bar of satisfied clients or articles about the business (< 6 logos)
7. How it works (3 steps; each step is less than 8 words)
8. Testimonials (< 4 quotes of about 8–12 words or video)

PRODUCT/SERVICE OFFER

1. Product and service photo conveying its benefit
2. Three packages: good, better, and best level—package names to be customized
3. Testimonials (< 4 quotes of about 8–12 words or video)

ABOUT US

1. Origin Story (< 100 words)
2. Founder and key staff photos and bios (< 200 words)

CONTACT US

1. Include form
2. Add map if you have a physical location
3. Email or phone number if available

Prototype Testing and Iteration

This step is where reality meets your best intentions, where the rubber meets the road. Show your prototype to potential users explaining that you are working on a project for a company and need their honest feedback. Do not indicate that this is your service or product idea because you want to get as much objective information as you can. Start with in-person surveys and document prioritized wants so you can complete a systematic analysis later. Over time, make changes that make sense. For physical products, watch how users interact with the product once you hand it to them. Ask them how they would use the product. Eventually, get their insight on the product website. For online products or services, share the wireframes or the website. Watch how they interact with the website and get feedback.

Create a preliminary budget that includes the cost of making the service or product by listing all the costs. Guess how much the product could sell for by looking at comparable offerings on the market. Don't overthink the first draft as it will likely change once the pilot happens.

User Analysis

Based on the feedback, now you can translate customer needs and wants into service or product features.

1. Categorize and prioritize the user needs into uses, likes, dislikes, and suggestions.
2. Be as specific as possible, using affirmative statements so they are easier to translate into features.
3. State what the product can do, not how it does it or what the user can do with it.
4. Group similar needs using cards, stickies, or spreadsheets so you can eliminate repeated or identical needs.
5. Prioritize the groups and translate them into feature improvements.
6. Make revisions to the prototype and supporting website.
7. Test with users until suggestions about the features are greatly diminished and the service or product is completely dialed in.
8. Based on the user analysis, crystallize what the emotional message is in six words or less and list the three to five most important features. Choose a visual—likely a photo—that best represents this emotional message to use in marketing collateral. This message will be what makes your service or product different from others like it.

Test the User Path

Let's reexamine the user path—how the user finds the service or product based on the user journey, the revised user profile, and the message.

Traditionally, a product's user path is often defined as a company selling to a wholesaler, which promoted and then resold to a retailer, who sold to the end consumer. The internet has changed the way product manufacturers go to market as they sell through online retailers like Amazon or sell directly to consumers through their own websites. In addition, services were often promoted and sold through resellers who had client relationships.

Going forward, the user path definition is broadening where service or product providers promote through various online mechanisms—social media advertisers, Google Adwords, bloggers, influencers, Facebook groups, and marketplace platforms—and sell through their own website. Many entrepreneurs list that word of mouth is the best promotion; this is true. However, word of mouth requires critical mass and additional input from other means to sustain and grow.

Map out what the user path looks like for your service or product. One end should be your enterprise while the other end is the end consumer. Include the intermediate steps, which could include online mechanisms or in-person influencers. Test all possible mechanisms out by investing $20–$50 on campaigns and see if there is a sufficient return on the promotion investment. Be open to trying alternative promotion methods—Facebook groups, Meetups, anything where there is a catchment area for potential users—as it may become your long-term competitive advantage.

Conduct Pilot

The final stage of the validation phase is to execute a pilot program, and its main goal is to demonstrate that you can profitably deliver the service or product to users who actually want your offer. The pilot is used to determine the sales cycle, which defines the number of prospects, user conversion rate, reorder rate, and referral rate. The deliverables include the following:

Number of prospects—Estimate the total number of potential users.

User conversion rate—Divide the number of actual users by the total number of prospects.

Reorder rate—Forecast how many users you expect to keep going forward.

Referral rate—Estimate the percentage of users who will recommend your service or product to another potential user.

User lifetime value—Show the value of each user based on their purchases. Estimate the total value of their purchases.

User acquisition costs—Show the cost of finding and converting users. This is usually determined by adding up all the promotion costs and dividing that amount by the number of new users.

Gross profit—Sales less direct costs of the service or product.

Based on these figures, you can demonstrate the user value compared to the user acquisition costs and the service or product costs. This exercise is foundational in deciding whether your business works. The aim is for there to be enough profit—money coming in versus going out—to also cover your overhead expenses like your salaries and office and administration expenses. If these goals are achieved, then a successful pilot will go a long way to convince yourself and potential investors that the enterprise is worth spending more time and money on.

Conclusion

Keep in mind that pilots rarely go as well as expected. The process is to pivot the idea or execution to improve outcomes. Multiple pilots may be necessary, though hopefully other projects. The goal is to demonstrate evidence that a profit can be made by offering the service or product to the user.

10

Accelerate

Accelerate

Let's focus on how to drive the enterprise forward now that we have proved the idea with users and stakeholders. These are the next key steps:

1. Promotion and distribution—Develop a plan and budget to build user awareness and the sales channel.
2. Developing collateral—Create compelling and consistent marketing materials.
3. Sales cycle and management—Map out sales metrics and determine the needed sales force and deliverables.
4. Scaling operations—Build out operating, administration, and financial support to grow the business.
5. Managing and leading—Create systems to grow the needed human resources.
6. Budgeting—Forecast money coming in versus going out.
7. Fundraising—Develop plan in order to scale its growth.

Promotion and Distribution

Let's update your enterprise's user path. This path is how the user finds the service or product, typically through various online mechanisms—social media advertisers, Google Adwords, bloggers, influencers, Facebook groups, or marketplace platforms—and the sales channel.

Create a map of how much you expect to invest in the various mechanisms and what percentage of sales will be sold through various channels. This exercise will help determine your sales and marketing effort and budget.

Developing Collateral

The marketing collateral formats will be determined by the promotion and distribution channels you plan to utilize. Most likely, the key marketing tool is your website with a combination of online and print. Online tools include organic social media (Facebook groups, Instagram, and Twitter), social media advertising, Google Adwords, and email. The most common print collateral is a 5 × 7 or 4 × 6 postcard to hand out at events.

All collateral should share the same key benefit and origin story. Be consistent in using the same picture, also called an anchor visual, which conveys the feeling of the key benefit. Develop a library of ninety-second videos, images, and descriptive text to refresh images and content on future campaigns. The visuals should be specific and memorable. Check out templates at Canva.com or Adobe Spark Page.

Sales Cycle and Management

The sales cycle includes identifying prospects, converting a percentage to buy, and retaining a percentage to continue buying. Given the promotion and distribution plan, estimate the number of prospects, user conversion rate, reorder rate, and retention rate for each path. Hold your sales force and yourself accountable to these metrics.

Let's consider your sales process. In the first six to twelve months, you will likely be directly selling in person or online to potential users. You will quickly learn what sales content and methods work best. Along with valuable direct feedback, you are able to confirm conversion, reorder, and retention rates.

When scaling, you will likely grow online marketing efforts by increasing investments in the methods that have demonstrated success in the pilots. If you have a service or product that requires in-person sales, consider these two methods:

1. Direct sales reps—This option includes hiring sales reps to call on potential clients or users. The user life-cycle value needs to be higher in order to support paying sales reps. This way can be both costly and complicated, but the method delivers the greatest level of control. It is best to check what other competitors are offering in terms of base salary and commission. In the beginning, you can check if the rep would consider taking 100 percent commission if the commission rate is higher than normal.

2. Independent reps/Distributors—This choice usually entails paying a 5–30 percent commission rate to non-employee sales reps who sell adjacent products in a particular territory. For example, if a coffee sales rep is already selling into coffee shops, a chocolatier may be able to convince the rep to sell chocolate bars into those same accounts. The trade-off is that you only pay commission because the rep's attention is split with other vendors' services or products.

Getting the promotion and sales channel right is a make-or-break decision for the company.

Scaling Operations

Marketing and sales are the tip of the business spear. However, the operations—product/service development and management, customer service, finance, admin—are critical to creating a lasting business. Operations tends to be very specialized based on the industry segment. This topic is beyond the scope of the book. However, finance and admin are often more generalized. The key is to get an online financial system that is highly scalable as soon as possible. The learning curve is steep but maintenance is straightforward. I suggest an online HR platform with some in-person support for set up. Admin—managing office, paying bills, organizing meetings—is probably a good place to spend a little extra money. A senior admin person can minimize startup drag, cutting down execution time and expenses. Virtual assistants can be explored if most of the work is remote.

Managing and Leading

The key to great management is aligning a company's resources to its needs. Unsurprisingly, people are the most valuable resource. The first five employees will likely make or break the business. Here are the steps to properly align your human resources with your enterprise needs:

1. Map and prioritize the main processes—Write out the five to seven most important business processes and draw a square around each. Under each process, list the key objective of each task. Underneath, list the key steps in each of the processes. Prioritize the steps from most valuable to least. Give some thought to how you should allocate your team's time and your own. Most of your time should be spent on those most valuable steps; outsource those lower-value-added activities. In the beginning, you may not be able to afford hiring someone to do those tasks. Consider using interns or hire lower-cost contractors so you can focus on growing sales.

2. Develop project plans—Using the main processes and their key steps, develop project plans, which include task summaries, task owners, deadlines, and graphics or charts to visually understand relationships. These plans will help you and your team understand what needs to be done when. These plans are the backbone to organizational accountability and help create a "talk the talk, walk the walk" culture.

3. Create job descriptions—Copy the key process objectives, tasks, and deadlines to create a first draft of different job descriptions. In addition, add a section for a personal development plan where you can document how employees want to improve professionally. Start with creating your own job description. It represents a realistic plan of what needs to happen in the next year where everyone is on the same page. Happiness requires shared, realizable expectations. Talk alone will not be sufficient as there will always be misunderstandings, particularly in high-stress situations. Based on these job descriptions, do online and in-person research on what the market rate is for the different positions. Create a range and check to see if it fits your budget. Realize that you will likely have to give up equity to bring on talent if you do not have enough cash. Potential employees may

join the team if they share your passion and mission, but they also need to pay their bills.

4. Conduct strong interviews—Great interviews require excellent preparation, which includes having clear job descriptions and reviewing resumes. Build a rapport by starting with easy questions. Be both courteous and firm. Ask challenging questions about their work history, skills, and how they have handled setbacks.

Ask what their salary expectations are. After thoroughly learning about them, give them a summary of the company and what your needs are. Give them an opportunity to ask hard questions so you can learn how they operate. Look for solid contributors rather than superstars. You and your fellow founders are supposed to be the superstars. Keep in mind that you will likely have to design around any individual's shortcomings to create a solid, long-term team. Hire the superstar only if you factor in that they may only be around for a short time and they can deliver on some very important goals.

5. Keep the best—Retain your best employees for the most critical periods by making them feel highly valued and overpaying them when you can afford it. Meet regularly and efficiently with key employees to go over process plans. These meetings could be as short as five minutes weekly. Have structure and regular communication to create organizational accountability for both you and your employees. Review and update all job descriptions each quarter. Cocreate each employee's personal development plan and be willing to pay for training if you can afford it. Employee retention is much easier when you are open to helping employees achieve their personal goals. Be honest that you will do your best to balance company goals and their personal goals.

Aim for balance in being a firm and friendly boss. Most inexperienced managers play the tough boss or friend boss role. Share the project plans and hold everyone accountable, including yourself. Keep in mind it is nearly impossible to be both friends and the boss. Know your employees' personal goals and interests and do your best to support the company's interests and that of the employees every day. It's hard.

Leadership

There are libraries full of books on leadership. Here is the least you need to know to lead well in a startup.

1. Have a clear plan—A plan forces you to understand the needed details while serving as a great communication tool to get everyone on the same page. Keep in mind that as things change the plan needs to adapt to new requirements.

2. Demonstrate passion—You have to be the emotional leader even when you don't feel like it. Bring it every day. Excitement is contagious. The passion and drive will power the organization past the tough times. You will have setbacks. Adjust the plan with enthusiasm and share with your team.

3. Build trust—Create a culture of "talking the talk, walking the walk." If you say you will do something, then do it. Hold your employees to the same standard.

4. Confront problems quickly—When you have a problem with an employee, de-escalate the situation. Step away from the office and give it some thought. Then meet with the employee privately using the following process:

   a. Start with a direct statement: "I have a problem with ____."
   b. Explain your position: "This is why I have a problem with ____"
   c. Ask them to work with you: "How can we solve this problem together?"

Be prepared to have a tough or awkward conversation. Better to have the talk before things fester and build. This skill is one of the most valuable in management and life.

5. Change your mind—Be prepared to change your mind if you get better information. By definition, you will be wrong often as you go through the idea validation and growth process. It's not about you but making the business work.

6. Empower your staff—When your employees gain your trust, have them take more ownership in projects. In the beginning, you will likely be creating project plans. Over time, ask employees to create the project plans that you then approve. Eventually, you can give them goals and they can manage the project plan on their own. Delegate decision-making where you don't have to agree with every single way they manage a project. However, intervene when you absolutely feel it is needed by framing the situation by asking questions that may lead them to your line of thinking.

These actions serve as a strong foundation no matter what your leadership style is.

Budgeting

Budgeting is a big weakness for most entrepreneurs. Most do not have the experience or skills so they do not create a robust budget. Or if they do create a budget, they do not update it regularly. Think of a budget as a scoreboard that lets you know how you are doing compared to your plan. The goal is to have more money coming in than going out.

Expenses are generally easier to forecast. List your expense items. If you don't know them all, reasonably guess after asking other small business owners or looking online. Revenue forecasts are hard. The best place to start is with your sales cycle metrics including the number of potential users, user conversion rate, reorder rate, referral rate, and user lifetime value. The only way to get better with budgeting is to do it again and again. In the beginning, it may be best to have a friend help set up a budget and then for you to take ownership of it. It is important for key employees to understand the budget and how it relates to their job responsibilities.

Fundraising

Raising money is rarely easy. The process is generally longer than you want it to be and filled with setbacks. Prepare for a long runway. The goal is to develop the best budget you can. Take the investment amount required in the budget and add 20 percent; businesses always require more capital than you think they will. Here are the best ways to raise capital:

1. Find ways to cut your budget as much as you can. Find lower-cost ways of doing things. Then add a buffer for unexpected surprises.

2. Try to presell your service or product to finance your startup. Find a first client or group of users using a rough prototype. A crowdfunding campaign can be hugely helpful though most campaigns work only if you are able to raise over 50 percent of the funds from people you know.

3. Ask suppliers to get paid after you get paid or try revenue sharing. This option will help drive down the initial investment amount.

4. Borrow money from friends and family. Only borrow the money if they are clear that they could lose all of the money and be alright. Give them a passionate and honest pitch. You could try pitching to banks, but they require collateral such as equipment, a house, or land. This choice is not

usually possible for most entrepreneurs. Many entrepreneurs finance their business with credit cards, which is highly risky.

5. Sell ownership in your company. This entails selling shares for money or issuing a convertible note, which is a loan that can be exchanged for shares at a later date.

Here is how the process works:

a. Prepare a package that includes an investor presentation, budget, working prototype, and pilot results.

b. Develop a potential investor list, which includes friends and family and other investors with a track record in investing in these types of businesses. Send out an email and a one-page executive summary.

c. If there is investor interest, get a signed nondisclosure agreement (NDA), which is a document that states that neither party will disclose trade secrets that are discussed. Once the NDA is signed, send the documents or make a presentation to prospective investors. Arrange follow-up meetings to get a prompt response.

d. If the investor expresses interest, then send a term sheet, which is a summary of the deal details. If key terms are agreed upon, then engage a lawyer to prepare a share purchase agreement and shareholder's agreement. Once the agreement is negotiated and signed, the investor wires the money within two weeks.

Negotiating term sheets and documents is an emotional roller coaster. Founders often confuse the company's valuation with their own personal worth. Investors are looking to buy the best deal, often perceived as a zero-sum game. Everybody wants to win. Deals often fall apart. A deal is not done until the wire transfer is received. Then the real work begins. The funds are just the fuel to actually grow the business.

11

Final Thoughts

In this book, we have explored the highest-potential growth areas and a process for validating those opportunities.

What Would I Do Differently?

I often get asked this question. For years, the answer was nothing—this was the path that got me where I am. I am an innovator, so I want to recognize reality as quickly as possible and adapt. Therefore, I have to be honest in assessing my past decisions.

Fly-fishing is not known as a life-threatening sport until it is. The month before the birth of our first child, my wife gave me a free pass to go anywhere in the world for three weeks. I chose New Zealand's South Island to go fly-fishing and smoke a box of Romeo y Julieta Cuban cigars. A cigar each evening represented the passing of one day until the beginning of my new life as a parent. I hired guides because catching trout in New Zealand was the PhD of fly-fishing. After sighting a rising fish, an angler only gets two or three casts to place the dry fly on the crystal clear, fast-moving water. The strong winds made for very few successful casts.

Midway during the trip, a guide had sighted a fish. I casted the fly eighteen inches above the nose of the trout. The trout sipped the fly and I set the hook. My reel screamed as the trout took off for thirty yards across the fast-moving river. I gritted my teeth, kept pressure on the rod, and slowly retrieved the line. I could not pull too hard or the tippet line would break. The old, bearded guide sat down on the bank to watch the chess match between man and fish. I was about to net the fish when it torpedoed away from me. My heart raced as I started to play not to lose. The guide yelled, "Chris, don't forget to enjoy yourself." I forced a smile, tried to relax, and worked the plan. After another five minutes, I landed the trout, had a quick picture taken, and released the fish.

By the next day, I had forgotten about the experience. The day after that, I was with another guide looking for more fish. It was raining, and we were inching forward in a new SUV along the bank of a ravine about thirty yards above a river. In an instant, the soft mud gave way and the SUV flipped over toward the river. The guide was able to climb out of his window. Though I had hit my head, I had the good sense to first hand him the fly rods and gear. Then I climbed out. Fortunately, the ravine held the SUV until a tow truck arrived to pull it to safety. It was totaled. I fared better. At the hospital, they patched me up with only moderate neck strain.

That evening, as I smoked a cigar, I realized that there is a beginning, middle, and end to everything. Sometimes, the end happens faster than you think. It struck me that my son could have grown up without a father. I reflected on how self-absorbing startups can be. I had forgotten to enjoy the process even when I was doing something I truly loved. I worried too much when things did not go to plan. Truth is, nothing really ever goes to plan. I came to learn to either enjoy the process or do something else.

I have come to believe that I am one of the most fortunate people on this planet if I have the opportunity to choose to do a startup that I am passionate about. I don't take that gift lightly. Even if the startup fails. At least I am in the game with a chance to win. Now, I enjoy the complete process: I enjoy the small victories as well as the little steps that others won't even notice.

Biggest Surprises

Here are the greatest surprises by which I learned the most. My life experiences forced me to rethink how in reality . . .

Nothing Goes as Planned

The truth is that nothing ever works out like you think it should. If you are dogmatic about life and business, you are setting yourself up for failure. I strongly believe that you need to have some core principles and values. However, in execution, you have to be adaptive. This quality is why the human species has flourished and why you can, too. You should plan the work. Work the plan. And be prepared to pivot. The only way you will be able to pivot quickly is if you have planned the work. When I was younger, I always planned. When things didn't go to plan, I would worry. That compromised my ability to adapt quickly. Now, I unburden myself of these expectations.

Hard Work and Being Smart Sometimes Get You Nowhere

When I started, I assumed that I would get ahead if I worked harder and smarter than everyone else. But life does not always have a Hollywood ending where the protagonist happily rides off into the sunset. The truth is that you will have to work hard and be smart. However, you will also need a little luck at the right time. You push the boulder up the hill. At some point, though, the soft mud will have to give so the rock goes over the mountain. The business needs to lift by itself at some point.

Sometimes, you will have to quit because the juice is no longer worth the squeeze. You hear the marketing mumbo jumbo that winners never quit and quitters never win. The concept works great for selling basketball shoes. Your season is a lifelong experience, not just one game. You learn from your losses and get ready for the next game. The ball has to bounce your way sometimes. You have to be ready on the field.

Patience Is More Important Than You Think

My second favorite Chinese fable is about a farmer who would pull rice stalks out of the paddy to speed up how the rice grew. Startups take time. Customers need time to get the offer. I often find my ideas too early for the market. In those cases, everything takes longer and costs more than you think. I have to try to make the runway as long as I can by surviving until the ideas are monetized.

You Don't Know . . .

My favorite Chinese fable is about a poor old farmer during the Warring States period. One day a beautiful white horse appears. When the farmer uses the animal to help around the farm, his friends compliment the farmer on how lucky he is. The farmer says nothing. Several months later, the horse bucks off the farmer's son, crippling the boy for life. The farmer's friends complain that the horse is nothing but bad luck. The farmer says nothing. As warlords fought for land, they drafted the young men in the village. They all died in battle except for the father's crippled son. Several years later, the son would marry a local girl. The old farmer was able to enjoy his many grandchildren. The moral of the story is that you don't know what the outcomes will be until well after the fact. A success today may lead to a huge setback in the future. Or failure today may be foundational to your success. Time will tell.

My Checklist

Over the years, I have kept a secret journal of all the things I wish I knew when I was starting out. I have deliberately kept the list short and sweet so I can read it quickly. Here are some things to keep in mind to be successful.

Passion

You have to have an irrational attachment to the project. There will likely be times when you will face the abyss where everything can fall apart if you don't gut it out. Win that deal. Raise that money. It's different for everyone, but the pit-of-your-stomach feel is the same. Every seasoned entrepreneur knows that feeling. Most likely, the irrational attachment will bind you to the project even if you weren't able to make any money from it.

Opportunity Recognition

Reread the chapters to ground your understanding in sports entrepreneurship opportunities. Read articles and follow publications. Do your research so you become one of the top subject matter experts in that field. Look for gaps by understanding the constraints. Get a feel of timing because you will need a little bit of luck at the right time.

Network

As you become a subject matter expert, check out social media—LinkedIn, Twitter, Facebook, and Instagram—and establish your social media credibility with other thought leaders in the area. Become a known quantity in that field. Go ahead and reach out and communicate with the thought leaders. You may be surprised to find a potential partner or a validator of your idea. Develop a network with people who share the same passion but have different skill sets. Give some thought to how you can build a team of people who are really good at things you're not.

Capital

Start to save money to use in your venture. Develop those fundraising contacts well ahead of when you need the money. Establish those relationships now in order to have credibility when you really need the cash.

Pilot

Identify ways to pilot inexpensively. The goal is to get user feedback, prototype the idea, and then get more user feedback. Do a usability analysis to understand what people really want. Answer this fundamental question: Can you offer this service or product profitably to a big enough market?

Distribution

It's really important to start building distribution concurrently with your product development. It's really hard to sell a product if you can't get it in front of the customer.

Process

Be sure to use the DIVA process. Discover. Ideate. Validate. Accelerate. So many entrepreneurs have a great idea between their ears. Consider the one who asks her three best friends about her idea, and they all say it's awesome. Then she spends a bunch of time and money on the startup. She drinks her own Kool-Aid. When she launches the product, she sadly learns that the customer doesn't really want it or is not willing to pay for it. She has six months to pivot and, more times than not, the company falls off a cliff with not enough time or cash. Following the DIVA process would have helped avoid this sad outcome.

Startup Timing

According to several studies, the best time to start a business is in your mid-forties. You will have an established network, work skills, and capital. The second best time is in your early twenties; the stakes are fairly low but your drive can possibly overcome your lack of network and capital. Otherwise, start the business as a side hustle with trustable friends and realize there will be limitations.

Support

Be sure to have your family's support. Startups are really hard. Establish firm boundaries and live within them. Keep the relationships to fight another day. Don't turn into a jerk. Entrepreneurs often get a case of the I-am-the-center-of-the-universe disease. Take care of yourself and those around you.

In the end, this book is about determining if the juice is worth the squeeze. Answer the question by developing subject matter expertise and owning the process.

I hope that you pursue your passions. If you do, you will wake up every morning and feel like you're living the dream. I wish you the best of luck.

INDEX

Italicized page numbers indicate figures or tables.